PR

DECODE
YOUR
DARKNESS

"This book is an easy and engaging read for such a heavy and important topic: trauma and emotional wounds. Richards takes on a tone of being your friend, companion, and guide all the way through. She addresses key points to help the reader understand the effects and mechanics of trauma but takes it much further by guiding others into a very valuable trauma-processing journey. As a trauma specialist who has led my clients through a recovery process after severe and complicated trauma, I highly recommend this book to anyone struggling with unresolved emotional wounds and even significant trauma."

—JON VOIGT, Licensed Clinical Social Worker

"Navigating our own darkness can be scary. Richards gently takes her reader by the hand and provides beautiful, powerful guidance to face their trauma, feel and release their emotions properly, and prioritize their own healing and growth."

—TED SMITH, Relationship Coach and Author of
*Healthy Me, Happy We: Transforming
Relationships With Yourself and Others*

"Brimming with personal insight, E. K. Richards lovingly guides us to embrace our darkness so we can learn to shine. Packed with useful exercises, *Decode Your Darkness* gives us tools to live life authentically—the way we are meant to."

—ANNIE CATHRYN, Author and Host of
Soulful Series Chat

Release Trauma,
Reach Emotional Freedom,
and Find Your Light

DECODE YOUR DARKNESS

E.K. RICHARDS

Paperback ISBN: 9798985680201
Hardcover with Dust Jacket ISBN: 9798985680225
Case Laminate Hardcover ISBN: 9798985680218
eBook ISBN: 9798985680232

SEL042000 SELF-HELP / Emotions
SEL016000 SELF-HELP / Personal Growth / Happiness
OCC019000 BODY, MIND & SPIRIT / Inspiration & Personal Growth

Cover design by Matt Davies
Edited by Catherine Christensen
Typeset by Kaitlin Barwick

ekrichards.com

To Miss Scarlett

May you find these pages a
reflection of who you are and be proud.

CONTENTS

PHASE 2: INTEGRATING THE SOLUTIONS 69

INTRODUCTION

At the end of Disney's *Moana* is a scene that never ceases to resonate deep within me. Allow me to set the scene for you.

Moana, on a quest across the ocean, is sent to restore the stolen emerald heart to the goddess of life, Te Fiti, in hopes that it will bring the life back to her dying home island of Motunui. Moana arrives on Te Fiti's island after a long and arduous journey, only to discover that she must overcome an evil, molten lava creature, Te Ka, in order to restore the heart.

In the midst of the battle with Te Ka, Moana realizes that Te Ka is actually Te Fiti transformed by hatred and negativity. Moana knows that she must be brave and trust in herself in order to bring Te Fiti back to life.

Moana holds the emerald heart up high, and the sun reflects off the heart, sending a bright light straight to Te Ka. Te Ka is instantly entranced by its sparkling light. The monster's gaze is fixed to the light of the heart. Moana requests that the ocean let Te Ka come to her (yes, she can communicate with the ocean). The ocean obeys and the waters part, leaving a single path connecting the two.

Te Ka screeches toward Moana, and it seems as though Te Ka will reach Moana and overcome her with evil, but the world goes quiet around them, and Moana fearlessly forges ahead. In true Disney form, a song begins. Moana sings to Te Ka about how her stolen heart does not define her and reassures her that she knows who she truly is. (If you haven't seen this scene, search for "Moana, Know Who You Are" on YouTube.)

Moana stands tall while the fire and smoke surround her. Her song has stilled Te Ka, and Moana is able to replace the emerald shining heart back into its rightful owner. With the heart restored, Te Ka flourishes into a gorgeous, lush, colorful Te Fiti once again.

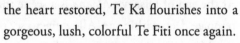

By embracing yourself as a whole, darkness and all, you begin to allow your soul the freedom to shine.

We are each Moana, Te Ka, and Te Fiti in one. The darkness that lives inside of us will be there whether we like it or not—whether we accept it or not. By embracing yourself as a whole, darkness and all, you begin to allow your soul the freedom to shine.

Life is hard. We all just do the best we can with what we've seen, what we've been taught, and what we're given in life. But despite our best efforts, we will inevitably experience pain and trauma throughout life. It's the human experience.

Immediately reacting to a situation or emotion is easier than sitting with it and working through it; so many people live their lives simply reacting from emotion to emotion or setting the emotions aside to avoid feeling.

As a result, we are plagued with anxiety, fear, depression, emotional numbness, and lack of passion for life. All of these feelings and past trauma automatically end up being dumped into that dark area of our soul. That area becomes a place where we can put hard things in the hopes of never having to deal with them. We think we are doing ourselves a favor, when, in reality, we are perpetuating the cycle of struggle and snuffing out the light of our soul.

You don't have to live your life numb and emotionless. Regardless of the trials and trauma you have been through as a child, a young adult, or mature adult, you can learn to embrace the dark area of your soul, understand its language, and give it an outlet.

Embracing your darkness is not an easy task—but it's so worth it. Without this critical skill, you risk feeling disconnected and directionless for the remainder of your life, unable to form a meaningful, secure relationship with yourself and others. Jumping into this adventure whole-heartedly will help you take the fragments of yourself and make them whole. You'll begin to see a bright future for yourself and truly show up authentically in your life.

BEFORE WE BEGIN
Where Are We Going?

In order to get to that ideal end result of authenticity, you'll need to trudge through some difficult things. Don't worry—I got you. So, where are we going? We are headed into the darkness. We are going to start with learning about trauma—yours, mine, and others. Once you've identified some trigger points for you, I'll give you some tools to work through the trauma and triggers (I told you—I got you).

Are we there yet?? Just about! We will wrap up our journey together by basking in the new you! You'll explore what you look and feel like after all that hard work and what your future might look like now that you've become one with your darkness.

WHY AM I HERE?

I was born into an emergency. Pulled from my mother's womb urgently. Sucking fluid into my lungs as I gasped for air. This was my dramatic entry into this world. Five pounds and nine ounces, nine days in the NICU, and then I was home. I'm not sure if this set the stage for my journey, but I'm sure it was, at the very least, a strong leading actor in the play that would become my life.

I knew from an early age that I was destined to change lives. I had an innate sense of purpose and an incredible gift of really feeling another person's soul. Later in my life, I would begin to identify as an empath. As an empath, I feel others' emotions as my own. I am naturally drawn to wanting to solve problems and heal the emotions of others.

Growing up, I experienced emotional, physical, and sexual trauma that produced emotions and pain that I couldn't or didn't know how to deal with at the time. Without the proper coaching as a child to express these emotions in a healthy way, I was left with mounds of bricks upon my small shoulders with no way to set them aside. So I hid the emotions and the pain away. I pushed it into a place that wasn't at the forefront of my mind. A place that I refer to as my darkness. I did this for an exceptionally long time. By the age of twelve, I had gotten incredibly comfortable with putting the difficult emotions and experiences into my darkness. So comfortable that I didn't even know I was doing it.

In my early teenage years, I started to crumble under the weight of those bricks. I began to feel the monumental burden of being responsible for everyone else's emotions. I cracked under the pressure, and my darkness began to leak into my everyday life. I began experimenting with ways to let my emotions out of their jail cell—some healthy and some unhealthy.

What happened in the following years was a beautiful disaster. A nice, long, leisurely journey straight through the deep, messy, marshes of my darkness. I manically wallowed in each and every emotion I had locked up. There was no start or stop, no rhyme or reason. I just felt—hard. I cycled through several unhealthy coping mechanisms to curb the pain. I lived my life in two dimensions—one where I would care for everyone else, shield the pain, and act tough. Another where I was a complete emotional wreck. (This primarily happened only when I was alone.)

In my twenties, after two years of physical health symptoms, I decided enough was enough. My body was screaming for me to unpack my darkness, and I was finally going to listen. It was clear to me that manically feeling my emotions wasn't enough on its own. I was going to have to explore each emotion and search for a root cause. I was going to have to take each experience and heal from it. I was going to have to learn to embrace my darkness instead of hiding it away. If I wanted my life back, there was no way around it.

This process evolved into a full-blown, one-on-one, get-to-know-you experience with my darkness. By trusting my intuition, I paved my way to healing. It took me almost another decade to navigate the journey to feeling truly alive. During that decade of discovery, I participated in intense therapy sessions, read a lot of self-help books, researched and tested numerous natural remedies, and did a whole lot of brutally honest soul searching. Now, in my thirties, I live my life with my darkness in mind—trusting that she knows what is best for me. My darkness is no longer a detached shed outside the home of my soul. My darkness resides within my soul, and it is as much a part of me as it is me.

This unity means that every day I show up as my true self—good or bad—through thick and thin. It doesn't mean that every day I radiate light and positivity and am the shining beacon of perfection. Far from it. It means that my presence in my own life and the lives of others is authentic. And when I don't feel I can be authentic, I take the steps to get back to myself.

Through my journey, I learned that to know yourself and live up to your life's purpose, you need to embrace that darkness, sit with it, let it overwhelm you, talk with it, and teach it how to effectively communicate. I learned through my journey that the light we emit can only illuminate fully with the help of darkness.

There are many ways that you can heal from trauma and learn to truly live again. Some are effective, and some are simply a Band-Aid covering the deeper issue. The tools you're about to learn will help you begin healing from the core. This is not an all-inclusive, "fix everything forever" book. However, the deep understanding of yourself that you'll gain from this journey serves as a fundamental foundation for further healing and continuous growth. You simply cannot authentically heal without this core understanding.

So . . . I'm here to help you let that darkness shine, my friend.

THE PURPOSE OF LIFE

"The meaning of life is to give life meaning"
— VIKTOR FRANKL —

Every single person on this earth has greatness inside of them. We were all born onto this earth with a purpose to fulfill. Our task in life is to live through that purpose.

When I say that we are all meant to fulfill our purpose, I don't mean that all of us are meant to come to earth and be well-known doctors, scientists, or life-saving individuals. There is a tendency to think big thoughts when the phrase "life's purpose" gets thrown about; but not all life purposes are huge endeavors or attract a lot of attention and praise. Your purpose in life could be to give unconditional love to your children. Your purpose could be to teach second graders how to write or to make people laugh.

There is no set size when we are talking about purpose in life. There is no parameter that the purpose must meet in order to be deemed worthy of its title. There is no rule that says that you can only have one purpose in life either. Some may come into this life with one purpose to last their entire life, and others may have many purposes. Your purposes can exist in solitary or in tandem with multiple purposes. There really is only one main requirement when it comes to your purpose in life. Your life purpose is meant to be something that fulfills you; makes you happy; and embodies the essence of your mind, heart, and soul.

We discover our purpose through all our life experiences. Life experiences serve to teach us what we do and don't like, what we are good at, what challenges us, and what sets our souls on fire. Throughout life's adventures, we create relationships, make memories, and leave an impact on the world.

Through life, we also get dealt obstacles that have the power to throw us off our path to discovering our life's purpose if we allow them to. Every life-altering event has this power. A breakup, the death of a loved one, a difficult health diagnosis . . . they come at us hard and fast sometimes. When you don't have the proper foundation to process the emotions that come with these obstacles, it becomes difficult to see the end goal clearly. The monumental weight of the event crushes your progress, blurs your vision, and stifles your growth. It controls you. By accepting each and every feeling as it is and allowing your darkness to compliment your light instead of control it, you open an amazing portal into your inner soul. A space for that purpose to come to life.

Discovering your purpose in life isn't always easy. Although for some it comes naturally, not all of us are so lucky. If you feel as though you are one of the unlucky ones, you're in the right place. It's so much more difficult to discover your purpose in life when your mind, body, and soul are out of whack. From this point forward, you have the divine opportunity to face life authentically and holistically. To live *inside* a moment instead of living through a moment.

> From this point forward, you have the divine opportunity to face life authentically and holistically. To live *inside* a moment instead of living through a moment.

ABOUT THIS JOURNEY

> "A story has no beginning or end:
> arbitrarily one chooses that moment
> of experience from which to look back
> or from which to look ahead."
>
> — GRAHAM GREENE, *THE END OF THE AFFAIR* —

This journey is not meant to fix you—spoiler alert, you don't need fixing (but more on that later). This journey is meant to enlighten you, to shed light on the dark sides of your soul and start talking about the hard things a little bit differently. To explore a realm of your being that you are often conditioned to ignore.

This journey will look different for everyone. My goal is to create a safe place for you to learn, explore, and grow. To normalize being a human. To normalize feeling. To let you know that you are not alone, and you are not wrong for experiencing whatever you are experiencing. Together, we will discover how to connect with your darkness.

I will walk you through some ways to face the hard emotions without going off the deep end. To do this, I've created individual tools called Darkness Deep DIVEs for you to use as you navigate this journey. They are a series of activities and reflection tools that I've placed throughout these pages where I feel you'll need them most. A lot of these activities are common in a therapeutic setting—and they are a mixture of tools that I've learned in therapy, through my time as a crisis counselor, and through self-exploration. These tools have all helped me at one time or another.

The activities are designed to help you explore your darkness, create clarity, stretch your comfort zones a bit, educate you, and give you opportunities to unpack your darkness in a healthy manner. A lot of these activities involve writing and reflecting. I recommend finding a space in your home (or somewhere nearby) in which to complete these activities. Your space doesn't need to be extravagant or decorated to the nines—it just needs to be available and conducive to growth and healing. A closet, a bedroom, a nook, a backyard, a friend's bedroom—anything will do as long as you can consistently return to your space and feel grounded in it. You'll also need a vessel in which to write—a notebook, a computer—whatever. Dedicate that notebook to your journey—you'll use it a lot.

> As a fellow darkness embracer, I'll share some intimate stories with you from my journey to embracing my own darkness. Because we are talking about the hard stuff, my stories may be triggering to those with similar trauma such as rape, self-harm, emotional abuse, or other traumatic experiences. Take care of yourself through this journey. Don't forget to breathe and love yourself. Set boundaries if you need to. Skip a story if it feels like too much. Have a trusted mental health professional on speed-dial. Pay attention to how you feel—that is, after all, the entire point of this book, right?

Think of this book like a hand-held, soul-searching, self-work sleepover without the nail painting and pillow fights. Okay, on second thought—this isn't like a sleepover at all . . .

PHASE 1

Discovering the Challenges

This phase is all about discovery.
You can't heal what you don't know,
so let's deep DIVE into discovering
your challenges.

CHAPTER 1
Defining Trauma

More often than not, I find that when I'm speaking about past experiences, using the word "trauma" often brings with it a connotation of a huge life-altering event. The "I was kidnapped and held hostage for five months before the authorities finally found me" type of event. Before we go any further, I want to crush that thought process.

Trauma is anything that overwhelms the brain's ability to cope, and it's different for every person. We all have our own unique thresholds for pain and difficult experiences. What is deemed life-altering for you may not be as threatening to someone else. That's okay.

We all have our own unique thresholds for pain and difficult experiences.

You can experience trauma anytime in your life. It isn't limited to the young and impressionable. Trauma will affect you regardless of your emotional stability, meaning that even though you make strides in processing old trauma and feel like you're in a healthy place, new trauma is not likely to just slide right off your back. Knowing how to feel your emotions fully does not give you immunity to life delivering you blows that knock you off your feet.

TYPES OF TRAUMA

The most common ways to classify trauma are to separate it into big trauma or big T trauma and little trauma or little T trauma. Don't let the name of the categories fool you though—little T trauma can be just as damaging as big T trauma. Either type of trauma can be a one-time experience or a repeated event.

Some examples of Big T Trauma are as follows:

- Rape
- Physical abuse
- Natural disasters
- Death of a parent
- War

Little T Trauma can look like the following:

- A breakup
- Loss of a job
- Financial stress
- Bullying or harassment
- Emotional abuse

In addition to these two classifications, there is also a type of trauma called relational trauma. It can be classified into the previous two categories, but I want to be sure to touch on this type of trauma specifically.

Relational trauma occurs during childhood when you feel unsafe, unstable, or unloved in your family, subsequently resulting in a broken bond between you (the child) and the parent. It can also occur in adulthood as a result of unresolved emotional wounds. It often goes unnoticed because it seems insignificant at the time or is normalized over time as you accept this as "just the way life is." Relational trauma also gets overlooked because it can be largely subjective. This type of trauma can occur as a result of any level of physical or emotional abandonment or neglect. It doesn't need to be on a large scale to be emotionally damaging.

I did a lot of empty knocking as a child. Knocking that was met with silence or abrupt dismissal. My immature fists rapped against the wood of doors separating my parents and my childhood so many times that even now, in my adulthood, knocking on an interior door in my home sparks feelings of rejection and abandonment.

My parents spent a lot of time behind closed doors for reasons that I can only speculate, and that don't really matter in the end. This separation was more than just a literal one. It created walls within my heart that degraded the bond between us. Many times, when I needed them, they were unavailable. This is relational trauma.

Maybe your parent or caregiver had emotional wounds of their own that they were preoccupied with, therefore shadowing your own emotional needs. Maybe you had a sibling with extreme physical or emotional needs that often outweighed your own, creating a feeling of being "less than" or forgotten. Having a parent that relied on you to take care of their emotional needs is a form of relational trauma as well. As children, we aren't equipped with the skills to navigate big, adult emotions—and we shouldn't have to.

Even though relational trauma manifests during childhood, it is commonly carried with you into adulthood. It's not unlike relational trauma to have a trickling effect on the way you handle situations, relationships, and parenthood in the future.

It is imperative that you recognize relational trauma within yourself and begin to hold it with the same regard you would hold any other type of trauma. Just as any other type of trauma, relational trauma has a profound effect on your mental health.

TRAUMA AND THE BRAIN

As humans, when we experience a threat, we have an initial physiological response to that trauma or threat. This was referred to by experts originally as the fight or flight response.

Fight or flight is an automatic physiological reaction to an event that is perceived as stressful or frightening. The perception of threat activates the sympathetic nervous system and triggers an acute stress response[1] that prepares the body to either become aggressive (fight) or run from the threat (flight). During this process, you may notice an increase in your heart rate, dilated pupils, tunnel vision, shaking, flushed face, and hearing loss.

As time passed and research findings evolved, additional responses were added to include freeze and fawn. The freeze response involves the brain becoming overwhelmed and ceasing to function, while fawn is the brain's attempt to avoid trauma and conflict through appeasing behaviors. Experts have also discovered that the brain's response to a threat can have different components as well. These include fright (fear takes over and reduces the ability to think clearly), flag (body systems begin to shut down and emotions are numbed), and faint (in extreme cases, the response to the threat is to faint).

It would be nice if the reaction ended once the threat was gone, but it doesn't. Our brains remember this threat and work to build defenses to protect us from similar threats in the future. This means that when you experience trauma—even if it was a long time ago—your traumatized brain can go right back into these responses anytime you experience a trauma trigger. In addition to this, until you find a way to help your brain process the trauma, your nervous system can remain at some level of fight or flight long term, even if there is no immediate danger.

Trauma and how the brain responds to trauma have a direct effect on physical and mental health.

TRAUMA AND YOUR HEALTH

Traumatic events change how our brains function and do the same with our bodies. Much of these symptom's stem from the constant state of fight or flight. Imagine if you were constantly fleeing from a predator—eventually your body would give out. Your mind would tire. Trauma can produce symptoms like

- Flashbacks
- Panic attacks
- Nightmares
- Guilt and shame
- Depression
- Feeling numb or dead inside
- Being on edge
- Irritability
- Suicidal ideation

The effects of trauma can also result in or contribute to many health issues, such as

- Substance abuse
- Eating disorders
- PTSD
- Bipolar Disorder
- Other mental health disorders

While we are chatting about the body, let me just take a moment to talk about the effects of unresolved emotional trauma on your physical health. In 2013, a twelve-year study[2] was published that suggested links between emotional suppression and early mortality rates. You've likely heard that chronic stress can contribute to diabetes, sleep disorders, heart disease, and other serious health issues. Bottling up emotions contributes to stress—stress contributes to health issues. You get it.

If you want to learn more about how your physical body and your mental state coexist, I'd highly recommend checking out the book *The Body Keeps the Score* by Bessel Van Der Kolk, MD.

In addition to the symptoms and health issues, trauma also brings pain. Once the initial threat of the trauma has passed, we are left with residual emotional pain.

RESIDUAL PAIN FROM TRAUMA

When humans experience pain, there are generally four ways we respond:

Solving the Problem	We seek a solution to the pain, accept reality, and remove ourselves from the situation causing the pain.
Accepting the Situation	We acknowledge that we don't like the pain or situation and decide to accept it at face value. We will either make the best of it or disallow the pain or situation to keep happening.
Adjusting Your Feelings	We realize that the situation is negative and decide to think positively about it.
Ignoring the Pain	We decide to ignore the pain or situation.

Since you're reading this book, it's likely that you've made the decision to ignore the pain more often than not. When you decide to ignore the pain and leave all of those emotions surrounding the traumatic incident unfelt, you may not be dealing with them immediately, but they still exist. Your trauma and pain don't disappear because you have chosen to ignore them. Your darkness is hanging onto them for you until you're ready to process them.

WHAT TO DO ABOUT TRAUMA

We've explored the realms of trauma, realized that we have experienced it, and ignored the emotions that came with it, *and* bottled up the residual pain . . . Now, what the hell are we supposed to do about it?

The first line of defense against the lasting effects of trauma is simply to *feel*. Learning how to feel and process emotions is crucial to your health. You cannot truly live without this skill.

> Learning how to feel and process emotions is crucial to your health.

Get to know the place you tend to put all the emotions and pain when it feels like too much. Get to know your darkness. Gain confidence in your ability to process the emotions that accompany your experiences going forward. You may not be able to control what happens to you, but you can absolutely control how you allow it to affect you.

Your trauma is valid. Your feelings are valid. There's no need to embellish or downplay the experiences you've had. They are your experiences, and you are right to feel whatever you feel about them. Take this permission with you as you go.

— DARKNESS DEEP DIVE #1 —
Creating a Trauma Narrative

Before you start the deep processing of your trauma and learning how to feel your way through it, you need to first accept that you've had trauma and look at your current trauma narrative. You may already be at this place, which is great! If so, use this activity to further explore some of the behaviors and symptoms you have as a result of your trauma.

Using the notebook you've designated for these activities, open to the first page and start writing your trauma narrative. I just want you to write down the story of your traumatic experience(s). This can be an emotional process—especially if you've never done it. I recommend having support with you as you do this introductory activity: someone you trust that you can call if you become overwhelmed, a comforting movie on standby, a tub of Ben and Jerry's, your dog, the crisis text line, whatever helps you recenter and feel better.

Start with the facts: who, what, when, where. Then you can move on to the feelings that surround the experience(s). If you have several experiences of the same nature, you can lump them all into one overarching experience, or break them up—whatever feels right to you. If you've had multiple traumatic experiences of different natures (for example, rape and abandonment) I would suggest doing a separate section for each one. You can compose these as lists or complete sentences and paragraphs.

For your conclusion, I'd like you to write a paragraph about your current symptoms and how you'd like to see your life improve. When you create a narrative for your trauma, you give your brain time to explore and accept it for what it was and is. This will give you an opportunity to identify emotions surrounding the trauma that likely still exist within you.

Below is an example of my trauma narrative when I began my journey.

When I was sixteen years old, I was raped by one of my friends, Tyler. We were hanging out at the home of a mutual friend, Colton. Several hours and a few drinks into the night, Tyler asked me to go into Colton's bedroom with him. We sat on the bed together and Tyler began kissing me. I allowed him to. The moment progressed quickly and despite my objections, Tyler had sex with me. He held me down and pretended he was being playful. He kept going when I asked him to stop. When it was over, I pretended to be asleep, and he left the room to return to our friends.

He drove me home in his truck at 2 a.m. Blink-182 was playing on the radio. I requested that he drop me off several blocks from home. I walked the rest of the way home.

The beginning of the night was filled with laughter and feelings of lightheartedness. When Tyler started kissing me, I began feeling unsure and awkward. I was full of doubt and knew that I didn't feel the way I was supposed to feel when you kiss someone. I was nervous to stop him because I didn't want him to feel rejected. I don't know why I let him take my pants off—it happened so fast.

The feeling of the blanket against my bare skin shot terror through me. I didn't want what was happening and it was going too far. I snapped into reality for a short period then. I told him I didn't think we should, and it was hard to say it. My heart was beating fast and hard, and I tried to get up. Tyler grabbed my wrist and pushed me against the bed. I felt confused and scared as he laughed and acted like it was a game and we were playing hard to get. I told him again that I didn't want to keep going. This time I felt trapped, terrified, and even more confused.

When he didn't relent, I succumbed to the moment. I felt detached from my body and could feel my muscles go limp against the bed. I escaped into the swirls and divots of the ceiling texture, feeling helpless and defeated.

At the end, I chose to fake being asleep. My body was heavy as I maneuvered onto my side, my back to him. I felt a sense of panic as I focused on feigning a steady, sleep-like breathing pattern. I didn't want him to talk to me, to touch me, to do it again.

When he left the room, I felt a sense of guilt and relief wash over me. I pulled my pants back on and laid there "sleeping" for several hours before I had the courage to exit the bedroom, rubbing my eyes, and ask to go home.

The drive home felt like a dream. The song was blurry in the air around me as I sat in the passenger seat of his truck. An overwhelming need to be far away from him took over, and I asked him to stop the truck and let me out. I told

*him it was because I didn't want my mom to
wake up with the noise from his truck.*

*The walk home was cold and filled with feelings of disgust, sorrow, anger, guilt, and more
confusion.*

*In the weeks that followed, Tyler bragged to
all of our friends about the encounter. He treated
me like a prize that he had won. A mountain he
had conquered. An object. I was filled with helpless embarrassment.*

*Right now, I feel lost, alone, and like I can't
control my own life. I feel like I don't ever actually feel anything positive—only negative. I feel
like my life belongs to everyone else, and I don't
know how to get it back. I want to feel good
things again. To have friends and family that
care about me and understand me. I want to
set goals and attain them. I want to feel whole
again.*

When I wrote this narrative, I thought that this was the
only trauma I'd experienced in life. As I progressed through
my journey and my mind began to open, I discovered other
traumatic experiences that I would need to work through.
This may or may not be the same for you, so feel free to
revisit this activity later on if you need to. When you begin
to explore your life, you'll start to realize how actions and
emotions effect you. After my rape, I felt numb. I was in
shock and didn't know how to process the emotions or the
experience. I was so confused at what had happened that I
just pushed the experience and the emotions into my darkness. I didn't want anyone else to feel bad for me, so I didn't
mention it to anyone.

When you experience trauma, difficult emotions are triggered. Then, either because you don't have the capacity to process them, you don't have the knowledge to process them, or you don't feel you are allowed to process them, you end up ignoring them and filling up your darkness with negative, light-sapping energy.

Releasing the facts and emotions surrounding your trauma onto the page is tremendously therapeutic. Not only does it clear your mind and allow it to process things clearly, but it gives your soul a chance to settle in and accept reality. All of this will help you as you delve into your darkness and begin finding yourself.

CHAPTER 2
All about Darkness

"Who looks outside, dreams;
who looks inside, awakens."

— CARL JUNG —

THE ORIGIN OF DARKNESS

Merriam-Webster's dictionary defines darkness as

Darkness – noun
    a: the total or near total absence of light
    b: the quality of being dark in shade or color.
    c: a gloomy or depressed state or tone

For our journey, I'd like to redefine darkness.

Darkness – noun
    a: an immaterial essence contained within a
       human soul.
    b: the integral section of one's mind that
       houses difficult emotions and traumatic
       memories.
    c: a guiding force behind the light and pas-
       sion of a human

Darkness was not always dark. At one point in the journey of our soul, all emotions were accepted and treated with love and compassion. We are born with a section of our soul meant to house our darkness, knowing that regardless of our situation, we would use it. We are meant to experience difficult things. These experiences shape our character and help to mold our soul into a complete human being.

During childhood years, we often received many messages in regard to how we are supposed to react, feel, and act. We became afraid and/or ashamed of our less-than-positive emotions and began to hide them from each other: whether out of fear of ridicule or rejection from others, or simply because someone once had a negative reaction to our truth.

Many times, we are taught that expressing fears makes you weak, that telling someone they hurt you will be awkward, that standing up for yourself might hurt someone else's feelings. We are taught that our physical health trumps our mental health.

The last thirty years have given way to incredible societal understanding in the emotional arena. As a human race, we are really beginning to realize that emotions and mental illness go hand in hand. That the emotions you feel have a direct result on your mental state. We are really beginning to pay attention to mental illness and give it the care it needs.

There is still much to be improved on in this area. Mental health deserves the same amount of concern that is given to physical health. There is still a lingering stigma surrounding mental health. It exists in the workplace when an employee dreads calling their manager to let them know they can't come to work because they're experiencing severe anxiety. It exists when your neighbor hides her depression because she's worried she'll be told she's "faking it." It exists when a teen doesn't seek help for his overwhelming thoughts of suicide for fear of being misunderstood or labeled.

There's a common root to this—fear. We fear the illness itself. We fear the reaction from our family members and peers. We fear for our future. We fear that we will be treated differently. As humans, we tend to attach some level of fear to uncertainty. Mental health illnesses come with a wide range of varying uncertainties: What causes the illness? Can a person choose to overcome it? Is it preventable or hereditary? Our minds do not work in the same cyclical, predictable manner as our other body systems, making it nearly impossible to attach black-and-white standards to mental illnesses.

I can't even begin to tell you how many people I've told my story to that end up feeling a sense of kinship with me because they feel a similar way. Yet no one ever talks about this. No one tells you that it's okay to feel like you want to cease to exist for thirty minutes out of the day and then feel okay the rest of the day. No one lets you know that sobbing in the corner of a party because you're overwhelmed is not abnormal. It is okay not to know who you are at a point in your life— or even more than one point in your life.

The unfortunate normal is smiling through the pain instead of embracing it and learning ways to give it an outlet. Pain should exist. It should be allowed to course through you, setting up shops

Pain should exist. It should be allowed to course through you, setting up shops inside of your body. It just needs a proper outlet.

inside of your body. It just needs a proper outlet, but more on that later on.

You were also conditioned throughout your journey here on Earth, both consciously and subconsciously, to hide the negative and show only the positive. Maybe you were like me and were not raised in an emotionally open environment.

Maybe you were taught how to express your emotions in a healthy manner as a child, but later in life, you were hurt by a friend, a partner, or some other individual and it caused you to backtrack and put up a wall to protect yourself.

Even if you had a trauma-free, "normal" upbringing, you still received messages that instructed you not to embrace those types of emotions. Just the simple fact that I can refer to these types of emotions as "less than perfect," "dark," or "negative" is proof that we are conditioned to be ashamed of these emotions. This is where pent up darkness is cultivated. Here are a few examples of this:

> **Situation:** An individual in your "safe circle" reacted negatively to an emotion you expressed to them.
>
> > **Message:** Expressing emotions hurts myself and others.
> >
> > **Reaction:** You hide your emotions to save yourself and others from pain.
>
> **Situation:** You received criticism from a caregiver or parent when expressing an emotion or having an emotional outburst—good or bad.
>
> > **Message:** Emotional outbursts result in criticism and more negative feelings.

Reaction: In order to avoid further criticism, you learn to hide your emotions and stifle your outbursts.

Situation: You don't receive the support you need after expressing your emotions to a trusted caregiver.

Message: You begin assuming that your feelings don't matter or that you're a burden to your loved ones.

Reaction: You start internalizing your emotions and/or look for other ways to receive support (not always positive ways).

Experiencing darkness is normal. Possessing ignored darkness for long periods of time becomes dangerous to your overall well-being.

THE PURPOSE OF DARKNESS

When I talk about darkness, I'm referring to the depths of your soul. The place that rarely ever sees any light. The location that most people don't ever see, much less really get to know. That is your darkness.

Let's get some introductions out of the way. Self, meet darkness. Darkness . . . well, your darkness already knows you. A little creepy, I know. Your darkness knows everything about you. All the things you would never dream of telling anyone, darkness knows.

Why do I refer to it as darkness? Well . . . because most of the time, it's dark in there! I mean, let's think about that place for a minute. It's difficult to access, it's hard to understand, it doesn't communicate clearly, it's cryptic, and, when it does communicate, it's generally depressing. That's all it knows! Because darkness is dark, it's difficult to see anything clearly when you're encompassed in it—especially yourself.

Emotions themselves are darkness's jam. That's what your darkness was built for—processing emotions with your guidance. Anger, hostility, depression, sadness, frustration, heartache, resentment, hatred. These are all normal emotions that your darkness is meant to deal with.

In addition to emotions, your darkness was also built to help process the event that surrounds the emotion.

Here are a few examples of the types of situations your darkness oversees:

- The depression that comes after losing a loved one to a long battle with lung cancer
- The anger and subsequent heartache that ensues when your partner of six years cheats on you with your best friend
- The insecurities you harbor as an adult after enduring years of childhood bullying
- The negative body image you hold on to because someone called you fat (or anorexic) once (or multiple times)
- The resentment you carry toward your parents because they didn't give you all the love you felt you needed as a child

EEK! That's a lot of heavy things for one single part of yourself to carry—and those are only a sampling of what some people's darkness embodies, mine included.

The inevitable difficult experiences you go through in life are the demons of your darkness. Childhood trauma, past traumatic events, relationship issues, insecurities . . . all these nasty little things live in that trench of darkness—usually for a little bit too long. They serve to stifle the darkness from doing its true job—decorating your light. They are going to do all they can to overstay their welcome in your shed of darkness, which is why right now, your darkness is likely filled with a lot of life's experiences that are hard to face.

There are healthy ways to utilize your darkness as well as unhealthy ways.

Healthy uses for your darkness:

- A temporary home for the tough stuff
- A quiet place where emotions go to rest before they get set free or converted into light
- A foundation of strength to build your character on

Unhealthy uses for your darkness:

- A permanent place to put the tough stuff so you don't have to deal with it
- A section of yourself to be ashamed of
- A crutch to excuse your unhealthy coping mechanisms

Your darkness exists to give you character and depth. It has an innate ability to digest the negative and exude the positive. We are all equipped with a portion of our soul that is dark simply because without the dark, we would not appreciate the light. It thrives only when you supply it with outlets to express itself.

Your darkness also has a specific job unique to you. Its job is to fuel your purpose in life. By listening to what your darkness is saying, trusting your intuition, and leading a path of authenticity, you'll find your path to fulfillment.

THE FACES OF DARKNESS

Darkness can manifest in a multitude of ways, both good and bad, depending on how you treat it. Since your darkness isn't necessarily meant for long-term visitors, ignored emotions shoved into that shed begin to take on an ugly face of darkness. This kind of darkness begins to speak out through your pain. It emerges when you are falling apart, when you are heavily resting on the rocks at the bottom of the ocean.

The ugly face of darkness doesn't like to waste words, so it only says what it means. It comes out to play when all your defenses are down and, a lot of the time, when you least expect it.

When you're ignoring your darkness, it's ugly face may look like some of the following: suicidal ideation, self-harm, addiction, unhealthy relationships, negative self-talk, depression, anxiety, isolation, narcissism, detrimental jealousy, severe social and emotional withdrawal, and the list goes on.

When you are aligned with your darkness, you are able to exist as your truest self. Authentic, confident, full of joy and passion. You're in the best position to live out your life's purpose. When you are misaligned with your darkness, it can quickly take over.

THE LANGUAGE OF DARKNESS

Each person's darkness has its own unique language. There is no school that we can attend as humans that teaches us how to speak to our own darkness. We learn this as we go, if we are a little bit lucky and a lot brave.

Imagine traveling to a foreign country where you do not know the language, only to be met with the added obstacle of the people of that country lacking the ability to speak at all. How do you learn to communicate with these nonverbal indigenous people? Your darkness is that foreign country. It can't communicate on its own.

I spent about six years of my adult life working as a veterinary nurse. During my time in this career, I gained a new way to communicate. A nonverbal way. My patients couldn't walk into my exam room and say "Nurse, my chest hurts, and I find myself out of breath when I walk to the mailbox with my owner. I never used to feel this way." I had to rely on my senses when communicating with my patients.

As humans, we need to learn to rely on our senses to connect and communicate with our darkness. This means we need to listen, pay attention, and reflect when communicating with ourselves. Mastering this skill allows us to connect with our true self and our darkness more effectively.

WHAT TO DO WITH DARKNESS

> "What we don't need in the midst of struggle is shame for being human."
> — BRENÉ BROWN —

I woke up in a truck. My boyfriend's truck to be specific. The soft, cloth seat pressed against my left cheek and my legs dangled haphazardly off the passenger seat. I wasn't buckled in, but we were moving. Why were we moving? How did I get here?

The last thing I remember is arriving at a party at my best friend Madison's house. Maybe there was an argument. Was I upset with her? My limbs felt fuzzy and weak, the way your foot feels when it's recovering from falling asleep. My brain is foggy and unsure as it attempts to navigate the nights events.

I remember, I was anxious when we arrived at the house. Not for any particular reason— just a lingering tightness in my chest and a rambling of thoughts rolling inside my head. I felt a constant, dull, ache in my left arm and I couldn't force myself to concentrate on any one thing. Madison seemed annoyed with my odd behavior. A flash of a conversation returns to me as I heave myself into an upright position in the passenger seat. I remember now, she told me I was being dramatic and attention seeking—maybe she didn't use those exact words. It's hard to pinpoint particulars. I try harder to reach the memories, but there's nothing there.

I'll never know exactly what happened that night. I can only rely on the recollections of others to walk me through my first black-out panic attack. In the days following the event, Madison did express that she felt as though I was faking what happened that night. I was crushed. How could someone that was meant to love me unconditionally feel that I would go to such extent to earn attention from others? Our relationship recovered but the shame and guilt I felt surrounding this incident did not (not for a long time at least). I became reluctant to share my feelings and symptoms with anyone—even those that I was close with. I powered through any anxiety I had and retreated to solitude when I couldn't control my emotions or my body.

How do you let yourself be dark when everyone is telling you that you need to shine? With such an intense social stigma surrounding darkness, negativity, and mental illness, it's understandable that you would be in the position you are in. It's not an ideal situation to self-sabotage, to wallow in misery, to let yourself feel only negative feelings all the time.

You're not supposed to make decisions that you know aren't good for you. We aren't given the social license to explore the depths of negativity when that's exactly what we need to do. I'm definitely not saying that you should act on urges to punch someone (or worse), drink yourself into a coma, or drive off of a bridge. What I'm saying here is that there is a happy (or unhappy) medium between ignoring and shaming the dark parts of your soul and accepting that everyone has a shade of darkness inside of them—and that it is *normal.*

We need to explore our darkness, to sit in silence with it for a while. To learn its favorite color and watch its favorite movie snuggled up on a black couch. It's time to learn that this is okay to do sometimes. It's your job to take care of *you*, regardless of what the popular (or unpopular) view is. The only way to crush the stigma is to prove that it can be crushed. Prove it to yourself first and foremost—you are worth it. Your body is worth it. Your future is worth it. Humanity is worth it, and if enough of us take this journey and trust in ourselves, society will follow.

Why am I acting like this darkness is an actual being? It is! Your darkness is an entire entity inside of your mind and soul. It carries all your deep, dark secrets. It feels all your emotions (sometimes all at once). It holds on to the fire inside you and keeps your passions safe. Your darkness deserves attention. It is time to get to know that darkness. Give it a name if you want! Have a few conversations with it. Explore its personality, discover its gender. Go crazy. It will be worth it. I promise.

I'd like to clarify this right out of the gate, because I don't want you to get me wrong. I am not asking you to morph into some black, evil hulk type and embrace a perpetually dark life. That would be less than ideal. My aim here is to guide you in the direction of training your soul to emit the darkness as creativity, greatness, light, and happiness instead of allowing your darkness to fester and emit as depression, lethargy, apathy, and anger. To integrate your darkness into your light so that your true self can shine through.

In short, what do you do with your darkness? You embrace it!

GIVE YOUR DARKNESS AN IDENTITY

My darkness identifies as a female. Her name is Miss Scarlett. She is prone to self-deprecating language and feeling like she is never good enough. She loves to emerge when there is a lot on her plate. She comes alive in solitary rooms with music deep in her veins. She lashes out when things are out of order—when things are not perfect. Her favorite coping mechanisms include self-harm and severe panic attacks—I am talking convulsions, numbness, chest pain, blackouts . . . not ideal. She thrives when her emotions are given an outlet—when I pick up a pen and let all her guts flow through my veins and emerge onto a perfect, clean sheet of paper. This is where she likes to live—right there at my fingertips, urging me to create. Miss Scarlett is fearless, unapologetic, and a little bit tactless at times.

> *Miss Scarlett was born in my mid-twenties. I was a single mom of a beautiful one-year-old, healing from an emotionally abusive relationship. I spent two weekends a month going out with my best friend, Lily. Lily and I were kindred souls. Longtime friends, both wounded, both mothers, both desperately seeking an escape from our realities. Every other weekend when our daughters were with their fathers, Lily and I would get together at my house, blast the music, bust out the vodka, and get all dressed up. We'd head out to our favorite local (kind of trashy) bar. We'd get drunk enough to sing karaoke and forget all about the lives waiting for us on Sunday evening. One Saturday night, after a few smuggled shots of vodka in the bar bathroom, Lily and I invented new identities. She would be Emmy, and I would*

be Scarlett. A gay couple from out of town, just out having fun. No one had to know who we really were, what we were like, and best of all, men wouldn't hit on us if we were there as a couple. We could just be. Our alternate universe lived on for several months, until the bar closed, and we decided it may be time to face our lives as real adults.

After our weekend excursions ended, Scarlett stuck with me. She became the idea that I strived to be—just me. She became a lot of things in the next decade: an esthetician, a makeup artist, a manager, a writer, and a wife. She evolved with me, and it wasn't until I was in my early thirties that I realized that Miss Scarlett was my darkness and my light inter-twined. I unknowingly gave her an identity and a life in one of my darkest chapters. I found a way to let her out, just a little bit; and although the way in which she was born was not the healthiest of ways to be born, she emerged, nonetheless. The creation of Miss Scarlett saved my life. The simple act of opening up a space for my true self to exist gave my darkness permission to begin the process of filtering through the pent-up darkness, honoring the emotions that hadn't been dealt with for a decade, accepting light, and living life authentically.

In order to live your own life authentically, you need to get acquainted with your inner darkness. Your darkness needs an identity—a way to escape. I recommend creating that identity now!

— DARKNESS DEEP DIVE #2 —
Creating an Identity for Your Darkness

Grab a piece of paper and a writing utensil. Find a comfortable place where you can focus and connect with yourself. Take a moment to construct yourself in your mind. Maybe you picture yourself standing in a room, ready to be built. When I participate in this activity, I always picture myself as a new Sim from the computer game. Standing on the pedestal with infinite possibility surrounding me. I watch from a distance as my creator begins to experiment with different personality traits. Hopes, goals, fears, likes, dislikes, astrological sign, career options.

Use your paper to begin writing down words or phrases that you would choose for the ideal "you" if you had the opportunity to build yourself from scratch. There is no wrong answer here. Write it all down, even if it seems ridiculous. Don't neglect the seemingly negative traits though— that is, after all, the purpose of this book, right? Write down all the less than ideal challenges you feel you currently have as a person. Trauma, limitations, attitudes, fears. You need them all to make a whole being.

Once you've filled your paper, give yourself a name. You can use your name, a version of your name, or a new name entirely. The name itself doesn't actually matter. What matters is the connection to the identity. This will serve as the identity for your darkness, giving you something a bit more concrete to coach, teach, and heal as you go along.

SIDE NOTE:

This doesn't have to be permanent. People change, and your darkness is no different. Humans evolve through life if we are brave enough to allow the evolution to happen. All the parts of your soul will evolve right along with you if you are connected. Repeat this exercise more than once if you feel you need to.

DOUBLE SIDE NOTE:

I know this sounds a bit like I'm encouraging you to become multiple personalities; I swear, I'm not. Sometimes, our minds, bodies, and souls just need a mode of communication to truly connect. The image of an actual entity embodying your darkness enables your brain to connect with your darkness easier. It allows for communication and clarity in regard to the part of you you're trying to communicate with.

Having the vision of a person with real emotions just like you to confide in and speak with gives you something and someone to recall when making life decisions and working your way through the tough times. I frequently ask myself, "Would doing this make my true self (Miss Scarlett) proud?" It truly helps me stay aligned with my true path.

EMBRACING DARKNESS

"Until you make the unconscious conscious,
it will direct your life and you will call it fate."

— CARL JUNG —

When you embrace your darkness, you discover who you truly are. Until that point, a section of your soul remains unseen, unheard, and unlived. It's common for children and young adults to not know who they are fully. That's when all the magic is meant to happen—that's when you explore, grow, and learn. That's when you begin to gain a concrete identity. However, when your childhood years are interrupted by trauma and abuse, that discovery is paused and put up on a shelf in order to face the demands of your current situation.

There were a multitude of reasons to explain why I had no idea who I truly was: I was young and still exploring my identity, but more important, at a young age I was not given the mental option to choose my identity. I was brought up in an emotionally unavailable household. The only emotions that were shown were those of anger, sadness, and turmoil. Being the great keeper of emotions that I am, I learned to shoulder my own needs and emotions and attempt to fix or take care of the emotions of others. My identity was a mixture of numbness and blind compassion.

For the entirety of my childhood and young adulthood I poured all my strength into the well-being of others and received guilt-trips, depression, and silence in return. I learned that when you invest in loving someone, they leave you. Or they never show up at all. This thought process would go on to define who the world saw me as.

I became the girl that never stayed in one place for long. I replaced relationships of all kinds when they became safe and scary—when they had a shot at hurting me, leaving me, or not showing up.

I didn't even know that this was not a healthy way to live. I subconsciously accepted my way of life as who I was. In fact, not only did I accept it, but my brain also found ways to transform reality into an identity:

Identity: I liked to be single and independent.

Reality: I was terrified to commit to someone

Identity: I enjoyed dating a lot and getting to know a lot of different types of people.

Reality: I was too numb to explore my own mind, so I focused on exploring others' minds.

Identity: I drink socially to let loose and have a little fun.

Reality: I used alcohol in public situations to calm the anxiety and not have to think about how to fake my way through a social interaction.

Identity: I loved to please others and explore my sexuality.

Reality: I had an extremely unhealthy relationship with sex because of sexual abuse.

All these things I convinced myself I was all about, without ever actually getting to know myself. I allowed my past experiences to define me. I allowed them to morph inside of me and become excuses for how I acted. But that wasn't the reality. My experiences do not have to define me and neither do yours. Your experiences can become merely pieces of your puzzle. Colorless, noiseless, emotionless. You can let them teach you lessons and provide opportunities for you to take many different paths in life. But, like a victim, you are not what has happened to you. You are the sum total of everything in your life. You can decide who you are instead of letting your experiences do that for you.

I know that you have heard this before: "I'm grateful for all of my experiences because they have shaped me into who I am today." I've also heard it too many times to count. I have even said it myself—too many times to count. Anytime I recall my "life story" in a deep conversation to a friend, or someone I have recently met, I say it. It's our way of proving that we've accepted the shitty things that have happened in our lives and have moved on, even though that isn't the case.

Yes, those experiences did shape you. They were the little machine parts that were carefully, methodically carving out the intricate curves and jagged edges of your pieces. But you don't have to be grateful for them. You can be angry at them. You can hate that they are a part of your life and something that you have to work around as you navigate life day in and day out. It's normal to not be thankful for the hardships in your life. You don't have to pretend to be this perfectly evolved human. You can just be your imperfect self.

What I am grateful for is my soul and my darkness. I am grateful for the strength that I have inside of me to keep going and keep growing and healing. I am grateful for creativity, poetry, and music that allowed me to wallow in my sorrow and float in an ocean of depression, regret, guilt, and numbness without judgement. My experiences have shaped my journey and will continue to shape that journey without fail or effort on my part. So will yours. Our experiences do not define us, though. I define me. You define you. Our actions and reactions define us.

The wisdom your darkness carries is immeasurable. It's able to hold all of your talents, passions, and purpose deep within it. Creating a best friend in your darkness will be one of the most lucrative endeavors you will embark upon in your life. Bringing priceless, never-ending lessons to you.

Your darkness can tell you anything you could ever want to know about you. It knows things that you do not even know about yourself. Some of these things will probably be hard to handle; some will be amazing, new things that you learn about who you are deep down. The good and the bad are both useful and essential in living your most fulfilled life.

Don't apologize for who you are. Don't turn back and give up when something negative arises from that deep dark dungeon. It will happen. Likely more than once. Embrace those negative things, become one with them, learn from them. Allow them to make you stronger and more experienced as a person. Let the negative things help you help someone else. Let the negative things bleed out on the page. Let them live through paint, ink, pottery, music notes. Whatever your medium is. Let the negative things live there. That is where they belong. Each part of us has a purpose and a home. Find each part of you a home.

SURVIVING VERSUS THRIVING

> "Thriving. That's fighting. . . .
> Surviving is barely getting by."
> — JILLIAN MICHAELS —

I remember the first time my ignored darkness reared its ugly head. I was fourteen years old, and after a few years of shouldering heavy emotions surrounding my parent's divorce, I finally snapped.

I don't recall the argument, or the specific event that frustrated or hurt me, but I do remember the door to my shared bedroom slamming from the force of my emotions. I remember the click of the lock on the bright brass doorknob, signifying a moment of safety, and then the messy clatter of my great-grandmother's small, pale blue mirror falling from its perch on my dresser and shattering into several large shards of glistening glass.

Sitting in a heap beside the shards, wrapped up in those four safe walls, the tears started to slip down my cheeks and fall to their death in my lap. My eyes moved to the sharp objects and without thinking, I haphazardly selected a piece of the shattered mirror and held it tightly in my fist. I could see fragments of my harrowed face in its reflection, and my arm moved effortlessly, guiding the glass to the pristine, bare skin on my stomach.

The weight of my problems seemed to fit so comfortably pressing down into my flesh. Like long lost lovers they united. The release was instant. It was as though every emotion, every single pain coursing through my veins was free. It no longer had to be caged and silenced. It could be heard and felt. It was as if my entire body was a bottle full of shaken, fizzy liquid and a simple shard of reflective glass had turned the lid in a counterclockwise direction. I was pouring out. I was hooked.

Cutting became my outlet, my release, and my sanctuary in one. This day marked the beginning of an unhealthy coping mechanism and addiction that would continue for several years. The first of many ways my darkness would attempt to communicate with me.

Self-harm is such a complex psychological coping mechanism. You would think that creating craters in your skin would be incredibly painful. For me and so many others, it's the opposite. Cutting created an avenue for feelings to escape an otherwise inescapable prison. It offered a much-needed release of the pressure building up inside my soul. It was akin to a life-saving breath after a near drowning. The blood released represented all the things I couldn't control and all the emotions I couldn't make sense of or sort through.

Employing extreme coping mechanisms is another attempt to survive. Your mind, body, and soul are screaming for help at this point. In order to help yourself, and begin to thrive, you need to embrace your darkness. If you've already employed coping mechanisms to maintain survival, that's okay. You can learn new, healthy ways to replace them. But first, your true self needs to learn to create a safe environment to marinate in your darkness.

You need to learn how to coach your darkness. To teach it how to communicate in healthy ways. You need to get to know your darkness: what it needs, what its breaking point is, and what it turns to when it has no support.

Doing this is not going to change who you are at the core, although it may feel that way. You don't need to change who you are. You are not a set of lost car keys to be found in the refrigerator. You know who you truly are deep down, and accepting your darkness and allowing it to enhance who you are will create a holistic version of yourself. It may look different than the version of yourself you've been allowing the public eye to see and that's okay. That's actually the point.

Just because you have a dragon inside of you, doesn't mean you are going to burn everyone you encounter. It doesn't mean that you must live up in the highest tower, disconnected from the world by a shattered bridge, protecting a princess. Maybe you're the dragon *and* the princess. You can be both. You get to be amazing, selfless, empathic, thoughtful, funny, and compassionate and still be selfish, hot-headed, and tactless; you can even make quick (not always the best) decisions. All of these things are okay.

Learning to explore the ways that you can express those not-so-good things about yourself without it affecting your life negatively is the fun part of the journey. By learning these valuable lessons and applying them to your life, you'll get to know yourself as a whole; and, as a result, you'll start acting, reacting, and communicating with authenticity and purpose. You'll begin to move from surviving to thriving.

Surviving	Thriving
Continuously allowing others to take advantage of your time, emotions, space, or physical body	Setting reasonable boundaries with others to protect your time, emotions, space, and physical body
Feeling like you're *always* tired	Having enough energy to get through the day, both physically and mentally
Constantly reacting to situations; moving from response to response	Thinking through each situation. Living in the moment
Impulsive actions (eating, spending, etc.)	Ability to effectively manage habits
Difficulty focusing	Mental clarity
Insecure, fearful, and/or excessively cautious	Compassionate, curious, and nonjudgmental view of yourself and others

There are several aspects of your life that come into play when we think about whether you are truly thriving and not just surviving. Let's take a bit of a shallow dive into these aspects before you deep dive into them on your own.

- **Physical:** This includes things like eating well, drinking lots of water, abstaining from drugs and alcohol, getting regular checkups, and wearing your seatbelt, of course.

- **Emotional:** This is what you're here for, right? To learn to express human emotions, love and be loved and live a fulfilling life.
- **Spiritual:** This aspect is all about standing strong in your personal morals, values, and beliefs. Being willing to seek meaning and purpose for yourself and your life.
- **Intellectual:** Feed your mind! Your mind needs to continually be challenged and inspired for optimal growth. Creativity and learning new skills included!
- **Social:** Everyone needs healthy social interaction (yes, even empaths). This aspect focuses on effective communication, healthy boundaries, and intimate emotional relationships with others.
- **Occupational:** Achieving occupational balance includes ensuring that you are utilizing your passions, skills, and strengths to enhance your life and the life of others. Striving for a sense of purpose and happiness.

Alright, shallow dive complete—let's move on to the deep dive! I'd like you to take a few moments to really explore the ways in which you are merely surviving and jot down some ways this aspect can be improved.

— DARKNESS DEEP DIVE #3 —

Choosing to Thrive

Grab that pen again (or pencil, sharpie . . . whatever) and get comfortable. This deep dive can take some brutal honestly if you haven't explored this until now. Get honest with yourself—it's the only way you're going to make progress.

You're going to make a chart similar to the one I made on page 50, but you'll have one chart for each of the aspects of life. It should look something like this:

Physical

Surviving	Thriving

Emotional

Surviving	Thriving

Spiritual

Surviving	Thriving

Intellectual

Surviving	Thriving

Social

Surviving	Thriving

Occupational

Surviving	Thriving

Think about each aspect of your life individually. What are some ways you feel like you may be surviving instead of thriving? Write each of those in the "surviving" column. Now take a look at that "thriving" column—what would it look like for you if you were to be thriving in this area? How can you improve your quality of life by making small, actionable, intentional baby steps? One thought at a time. One behavior at a time.

CHAPTER 3
The Light

"There is a crack in everything,
that's how the light gets in."

— LEONARD COHEN —

THE ORIGIN AND PURPOSE OF LIGHT

Just as we were all born with a space for darkness, we are all born with a space for light. Your light is a spot to house your positive traits, core values, morals, and passions. The purpose of light is to help you fulfill your purpose in life, show the world who you are and assist your darkness in healthily expressing emotions.

In a perfect world, your light would be the side of you that the world sees easily. The persona that exemplifies your true self and shines bright for others, leading the way to everlasting joy and happiness. We don't live in a perfect world though. Which means that the light you emit isn't always authentic. You choose to emit what you want the world to see. Sometimes consciously and sometimes unconsciously.

Just as your childhood experiences and teachings have a direct impact on how you treat your darkness, they directly influence how you treat your light and what you allow others to see. Let's take those same proposed situations we used earlier and explore their effect on your light:

Situation: An individual in your "safe circle" reacted negatively to an emotion you expressed to them.

> **Message:** Expressing emotions hurts myself and others.

> **Reaction:** You hide your emotions to save yourself and others from pain.

> **Effect on light:** You become resistant to expressing your authentic self (your authentic light).

Situation: You received criticism from a caregiver or parent when expressing an emotion or having an emotional outburst—good or bad.

> **Message:** Emotional outbursts result in criticism and more negative feelings.

> **Reaction:** In order to avoid further criticism, you learn to hide your emotions and stifle your outbursts.

> **Effect on light:** The energy you spend convincing yourself not to show your true emotions is pulled from the energy of your light.

Situation: You don't receive the support you need after expressing your emotions to a trusted caregiver.

> **Message:** You begin assuming that your feelings don't matter or that you're a burden to your loved ones.

> **Reaction:** You start internalizing your emotions and/or look for other ways to receive support (not always positive ways).

> **Effect on light:** The negative thought and internalizations begin to take over, causing your light and authentic self to become muddled and lost.

Your darkness and your light have an extremely close relationship. Even though they are technically opposites, they interact and affect the function of each other directly. When your darkness isn't treated properly, your light suffers. When you embrace your darkness and give yourself freedom to feel, your light is able to shine brightly. Think of them as sharing a duplex inside your soul. They live separately, but they share an entire wall of their dwelling with the other. Those walls are paper-thin and extremely permeable. Together, your darkness and light hold your zest for life, your dreams, your creativity, and your goals.

THE FACES OF LIGHT

Authentic Light

Most people think of this face first. This light is the thing inside of you that shines so brightly it cannot be mistaken for anything but exactly what it is—a beacon of hope and purpose. This is the face of light everyone longs to have, and the face I wish for you. Authentic light emits when you are acting as your truest self. In order for this to happen, you must have open communication with all of the sections of your soul—including your darkness.

> **What it could look like:** You're in your element—enjoying an evening with your closest friend. Together, you're making plans to travel to Costa Rica next summer. You're confident, comfortable, and genuinely happy. A far cry from where you were several months prior. You're looking forward to life and exploring a passion for travel that you've been too burdened with anxiety to explore until now.

> **Why you need it:** Authentic light is vital to living an authentic life—go figure. It's not necessary for your authentic light to shine all the time. In fact, it's not realistic to believe that it is supposed to. You are always going to encounter detours in life that challenge your expression of your authentic light. That's a normal part of life and actually what strengthens your authenticity. Life is about taking those detours, snapping a few pictures to remember the journey, and hopping back on that path to purpose.

When to turn it off: I can't think of a reason that you would ever want to turn off your authentic light (if you think of one, let me know). I can think of reasons that your authentic light would dim or turn off on its own, though. Fear, anxiety, depression, insecurity, suppressed trauma—all of the contributors and enablers to unhealthy darkness can cause your authentic light to dim or shut off temporarily.

Forced Light

This face of light emits when you've put a mask on. When you have decided either consciously or subconsciously that your emotions or true self will not be accepted by the recipients. Generally, this light matches its surroundings in order to better fit in.

What it could look like: You're away from home on a work trip, which already makes you nervous. Today is the final day of the convention you've been assigned to attend. You're seated at a table with several seasoned male CEOs, and you're feeling incredibly intimidated. You quickly put on your "game face" and interact with the men in a way that isn't true to you or your core values. You wouldn't want them to think less of you for being quiet, reserved, and simple.

Why you need it: Believe it or not, your forced light actually serves to cut the drama out of your life sometimes. It can also serve to save you unnecessary emotional upset. Remember when I told you that it was okay to just be whatever you were in that moment? Your forced light is a great example of that ringing true.

The reality is that sometimes it's necessary to utilize your forced light in a situation. Is it really necessary to challenge your mother-in-law at a large family gathering when she openly expresses her disapproval of co-sleeping with an infant, and you're two months into co-sleeping with your youngest? Maybe ... but also ... maybe not. There's no need to create emotional upset—your core values are still intact and so are hers. Go ahead and slap that mask on, smile, and say, "That's a great point of view, Margorie!"

When to turn it off: There is no need to keep a mask on when your core values are at stake. If you're in a situation that has the potential to affect your life in some way, your forced light should be in the "off" position. Let's take the same co-sleeping scenario and imagine that your mother-in-law has now moved to convincing your husband that you are a terrible mother for choosing to co-sleep with your child. This situation has just moved from harmless to harmful. Now is the time to take that mask off, turn your forced light off, and express yourself through authentic light.

Filtered Light

This is the light your soul emits when it's in protector mode. It can be quite similar to forced light, but usually this type of light is emitted subconsciously. It's your soul's way of keeping you from harm and heartache. This face of light allows portions of your true self to shine through, but only what is deemed as the safe amount. The remainder of your true self and authentic light remain hidden.

What it could look like: You're at your friend's birthday party when your abusive ex shows up. You're instantly uncomfortable and feel your chest tighten. Your brain has entered protector mode. You consider fleeing but you know that your friend would be hurt if you did. You know that there is nothing your ex could do to hurt you right now and that you're SO over the relationship. You're stronger, smarter, and far surer of yourself now. You stay at the party, but you just aren't quite yourself. Your laugh is partially stifled, and your movements and actions are measured.

Why you need it: Filtered light can be useful as a sort of "halfway house" to healing. When you aren't quite sure if you can handle the full extent of a situation or emotion, allow the filtered light to keep you protected while you slowly let your authentic light take over. You may need that filtered light until you are ready to face or process whatever you're being protected from.

When to turn it off: It takes time and patience to rewire our brains for safety once they've been in an unsafe situation. So when you get to the point that you've processed a trauma or emotion, it can be difficult to make the decision to turn your filtered light off. It's like taking the training wheels off your bike. There's a chance you're going to fall on your face once you do.

There are rare occasions when this light will automatically shut off right when it should. Right when you're ready for it to. But more often than not, you'll need to let your brain know that it's okay to stop using this light in a situation. You can let your brain know via a straightforward conversation with yourself or by consciously emitting your authentic light when you're in this situation.

Each of the faces of light serve their purpose temporarily and each face plays its part in making up the entirety of your being. They all work as a team to get you through life, which means that there will be times when all of your lights are shining in tandem—that's okay! As you examine and begin to honor each emotion, each trauma, each life experience, you'll start to get to know your light. Instinctively, you'll feel what your soul needs from each part of you and learn to care for it accordingly.

Just like wallowing in darkness is detrimental to your life, so is wallowing in positivity. I think it's important to touch on the positivity movement, or toxic positivity, while we are chatting about your light.

THE POSITIVITY MOVEMENT

"What you think, you become.
What you feel, you attract,
what you imagine, you create."

— BUDDHA —

The positivity movement is essentially the idea that positive thinking will yield positive results. The human mind is such a powerful beast. It's absolutely true that your body takes its cues from your mind. Optimism has a profound effect on healing, stress level, depression, life span, social life and so much more. I totally subscribe to all of these beliefs. I wholeheartedly believe that if you put good energy into the universe, you're going to get that back. I *know* that karma is a bitch. I've dealt with her firsthand. Positivity brings good things to your life. Negativity breeds negativity.

Here's where the positivity movement goes wrong: it leads you to believe that positivity is all you're meant to feel. With all the messages urging us to constantly think positively, it's easy to misunderstand this well-meaning notion.

Yes, thinking positively is a beneficial tool to have in order to pull you through the ups and downs of life, but what has happened is that we think that all we are supposed to feel are the "good" emotions. We've been conditioned to believe that the "bad" emotions don't serve us. That is simply not the case. It's not the positivity movement's fault—it means well. Nowhere in the notion of positivity does it tell us to ignore the negativity completely. But as a society, we have morphed it as such.

Attaching shame and guilt to feeling anything negative, dismissing yours or others' difficult feelings or obsessively reciting positive affirmations are all signs of toxic positivity. Toxic positivity takes positive thinking and puts it into hyperdrive. It minimizes and rejects any human emotion that isn't strictly positive, and it's a dangerous way to live.

Wallowing in misery and negativity for a prolonged period of time without reprieve will not invite good things into your life. However, the proper processing of negative emotions is necessary for the human brain, heart, and soul to truly live.

So, what happens when even through all those positive affirmations, you still feel dead inside? When you feel overwhelmed and trapped—like there's no way out?

You are suffering from the *illusion* that you are dead inside. Don't worry, you're not alone. You're also not *really* dead inside. You've just been conditioned by society and your experiences to bottle up your emotions, think positively, and move on. As a result, you've overloaded your soul to the point that it has shut down temporarily. That illusion of being dead inside is actually life in disguise! It just needs to be nurtured, understood, and converted into light.

You've focused on being such a positive light for so long, it feels like you're not allowed to feel or express anything but that light and optimism. It may even feel that you're going against your core values if you show weakness. Feeling the need to constantly be optimistic takes a lot of energy. Energy that is spent on pushing any negative experience aside and "getting through" the emotions that go with the experience so that you can get back to a state of positivity. That's an exhausting cycle. It is completely possible to embrace both your darkness and positivity, but you need to acknowledge your darkness first.

Imagine a life where you don't feel the weight of your darkness threatening to take you under. Where you are free to live authentically, without fear and guilt plaguing you. A life where you no longer feel the need to live according to anyone's expectations but your own. A world where you no longer hold your identity a prisoner of your own mind. But instead, you embrace your identity and allow your mind the freedom to feel and think freely. No judgement, no guilt, no shame. Just you. That's what happens when you let both the light and the darkness in.

INTERTWINING DARKNESS AND LIGHT

In the thick of my low days, I took a trip back home to see my dear friend and soul sister, Emily, get married. While on the trip, my father facilitated a visit for myself, my two sisters, and him to meet with one of his friends—a woman with a gift. While I don't recall her name now, over a decade later, the experience she provided was unforgettable. This woman's gift was feeling and seeing others' auras. She used this gift to help individuals through troubled times or to face past, lingering pain.

Going in, I was skeptical. Not because I didn't believe that people like her existed, but because I wasn't sure that she was really one of those individuals. How did I know she wasn't faking it? Collectively, we made our way to the door, and my father knocked. The woman (I'll call her the aura reader) opened the door and greeted us warmly. Within seconds of being invited into the entryway of her home, she let us know that she had been being attacked by negative spirits since confirming the appointment with us all. She explained that the spirits were attempting to stifle her gift and ability to see inside of us and to help us. The spirits didn't want her to help one of us in particular because one of us was meant to do great things in life: to help others and bring light to the world. The spirits wanted the individual to stay perpetually haunted.

She looked right at me and said, "I can already tell that that individual is you." Yeah... okay, lady, is what I thought at the time.

We sat down in her dated living area, exchanged full introductions and a few pleasantries, and she began with me. She started with some generic statements that you would expect from anyone—"you've had some hard times," blah, blah, blah. But she went further. She recalled specific life experiences and paired them with emotions that no one knew I had because I never revealed them. She went on to detail numerous things about my life and my soul that would be impossible for anyone to know. Some things that I hardly even knew. I became a believer then.

The aura reader began asking me things that I liked to do—seemingly simple questions, but I was torn for an answer. I had been so miserable for half a decade that I couldn't think of anything in life that I liked. My father chimed in: "She's a really great writer. She writes poetry." Her face softened, and she let out a large breath. "There it is," she said. "Until now, all I could see is darkness inside of you, but the moment your dad mentioned writing, your entire aura lit up. This is what you are meant to do with your life. Write."

Writing is my light. But my writing is fueled by my darkness. For years, I kept the two completely separate. I wrote when I was depressed, in a fit of rage, drowning in my own tears. I wrote when my life was hard and depressing. I loved the feeling I got when I wrote. A pain-numbing high that I only got when I shoved the earbuds into my ears, turned the volume up, and put a pen in my hand.

Writing was the outlet for my emotions when I couldn't express them verbally, but I could only access that outlet when I was in a bad place. I allowed my darkness to rear its ugly head only in the comfort of own solace. A place where no one could judge me for my horrible thoughts and actions. I would let my darkness run its course and speak through many unhealthy means and then I would pack it up, paste a smile on my face, unlock my bedroom door and return to the world.

When you live your life only focusing on the light and ignoring your darkness, the person that you put out into the world isn't really you. It is only a chunk of you. The chunk that you are comfortable with the public witnessing. The chunk that seems perfect. This becomes problematic when trying to cultivate authentic, deep relationships—romantic and otherwise. You'll find that you can't truly connect with many individuals because you are not acting as your true self. This will continue until you've taken the time to listen to your darkness. To truly listen to understand, you need to sit with it and explore it.

The key is to not separate the two. Darkness and light need to coexist in order to be their brightest. You need to be their guide though. To guide the darkness to the path that leads to light. Otherwise, darkness will turn to blackness, and that line between darkness and blackness is a dangerous one.

This is about blending the darkness and light—allowing the darkness to shine and decorate your light. This is about finding your purpose in life and living authentically. This is about feeling all the feelings. Your light and your darkness can coexist merrily, and I can help you with that. Your darkness can make your light shine even brighter, be even more resilient. Your darkness adds sparkle to that light. It adds character and experience; it adds maturity and a zest for life that cannot be beaten down. Now *that* sounds even better to me.

PHASE 1 REFLECTION

Use these questions to reflect on phase one.
Think about them, say the answers out loud,
write them down—you do you.

*What types of trauma have you experienced?
How has it affected your life (mentally,
physically, socially, spiritually)?*

*What did you learn from writing
your trauma narrative?*

*What is your current relationship
with your darkness?*

*How does your darkness
manifest itself in your life?*

*What scares you about
decoding your darkness?*

How often do you wear a "light mask"?

PHASE 2

Integrating the Solutions

Now that you've learned about challenges and roadblocks, it's time to learn about some tools for healing and how to include them in your journey.

Let's deep DIVE into the solutions.

CHAPTER 4
The Tools

TYPES OF TOOLS

Before we move forward, I would like you to have some tools just in case you need a helping hand on your journey into the darkness. Since I can't be physically present with you on this adventure, my advice would be to have a support system as you embark. For me, this means I have my person available to call or text if I need to escape. I have my safe place to relax in while I access these emotions. I have a toolbox full of resources to help me forge my path, and they are there in case I need to build a shelter along the way.

You may not need all of them at once. You may only use one of them, but you'll use it again and again. This journey is more of an art form than rocket science. Don't stress about having every single one of the tools right now. Focus on at least having one—maybe it's the one that resonates with you the most when reading through them. Maybe it's the one that you have already mastered. Just have at least one as we head into this.

As we progress, you can build on to your set of tools. You'll realize that some are better than others to deal with certain things and that some of them just aren't for you. That's all okay. You may even find a tool that works miracles for you that I didn't mention. That's amazing, I'm all about new tools!

A SAFE PLACE

A safe place is a location that you create in your mind. One that provides you with a sense of security, calm, and peace. If your mind can convince you that it's in danger or that bad things will happen, it can also convince you that everything is okay.

Imagine for a moment that every time something negative happened, you had a place to go where all of the chaos falls silent. Where you can breathe easily, regroup, and regain the strength to take on whatever lies outside the door. That's what a safe place is.

The cabin is my safe place. A room with a fireplace blazing warm. The soft crackling of the fire perfectly accentuates the chatter of a Hallmark movie playing on the TV mounted above the chunky wood mantel. The mantel is delicately adorned with ornate books and photos of me and my closest friends enjoying each other's company. A king-sized bed sits next to a large window, swarming with white, down bedding; and I'm happily drowning in the sea of down comforter up around my chest and shoulders. And resting on the pillows behind my head is my Schnauzer, Lucy (she's much too posh to sleep at my feet—a pillow is the only option). The window to my left is cracked slightly—allowing a slow, steady stream of icy, winter air to touch my face lightly. The air outside smells clean and crisp, but inside, the smell is a mix of chocolate, coffee, and fresh pine. Opposite the fireplace lives a wall of other worlds. White shelves of books to transport me anywhere I'd ever want or need to go. Nestled quaintly in a corner is a Christmas tree, magically lit with tiny, warm, white lights and adorned with sparkly glass balls. Here, I can marinate in the warmth of safety.

I come here often. Even in the heat of the summer months, my cabin sits waiting for me anytime I need to visit. My bedroom often transforms into this magical, safe place. My kitchen, my car, my shower—all have become a cabin at some point in time. My crying toddler disappears for moments in time while I bask in the warmth of Christmas tree lights. My safe place allows me an escape from whatever I need to escape. It's a home I can return to and a place I can come to process my emotions safely.

This brings me to the first of the darkness assignments in this section. This one is an important one, so don't move on without it!

— DARKNESS DEEP DIVE #4 —
Creating a Safe Place

Get yourself a cabin. It can be whatever you want, really. Get comfortable, take some deep breaths, close your eyes, and let your mind envision a place where everything is at ease. What do you see? What do you feel? What do you smell? Take some time envisioning this place. Use all of your senses and build a place in your mind that serves you well. Give your safe place a name. Make it real. Tangible. Repeat the name of your safe place both in your mind and out loud. This helps you to mentally transport yourself to this place in the future by using this auditory cue.

Once you have your safe place, start to use it. It won't do you any good when it's empty. It needs you just as much as you need it. I promise. There may be a time when your safe place is no longer serving you the way it once did. It's okay to create a new one. It's okay to create multiple new ones. You're going to grow and change through this journey and through life. It's understandable that your safe place will change right along with you.

MEDITATION

Feeling all the things is exhausting. It will always be exhausting. That is the hard truth. We need to give our minds a break. There are days when I cannot wait until bedtime so that my mind can rest. Then there are the nights where my dreams are even more realistic than my life itself; those make for doubly tough days. Meditation allows our minds to rest without sleeping. It's the practice of being in control of what our minds do. Your thoughts spend all day (and sometimes all night) attempting to control everything. They deserve a break.

Meditation takes practice, and if you're anything like me, you may get frustrated that you can't instantly grasp it. That you can't automatically get your mind to be still, and you may want to give up. I have been there—So. Many. Times. Keep trying. Know that you aren't going to master it the first time, or the second time or the third time. Rejoice in your mind settling even for a fraction of a second. That is a win, I promise. Eventually it will come, and the benefits will be plentiful.

Practice daily. Multiple times if you can. Practice in the bathroom, the shower, any time you have five to ten minutes. Just practice.

Here's a good place to start if you're new to meditation.

— DARKNESS DEEP DIVE #5 —
Introduction to Meditation

Find a quiet place. (Eventually you may be able to do this in a noisy place, but you gotta learn to walk before you can run.) Make sure you're seated in a comfortable position and take some deep breaths. In through the nose and out through the mouth. Which each exhale, allow your body to relax even more. Feel the weight of your body on the surface underneath you.

Relax your eyes as your breathing returns to normal. This can mean that you have a fixed, soft gaze or you gently close your eyes. Take some time to focus on your breathing. Enjoy the soft rhythm of the inhale and exhale. Notice where you feel your breath and what it feels like.

When your mind wanders like it inevitably will, gently bring it back to focus on your breathing.

When you feel ready, slowly open your eyes, or regain focus on your surroundings. Take a minute to bring yourself back to reality.

BREATHE

This one seems like a no-brainer, right? Clearly you need to breathe to stay alive and you can't exactly flourish if you're dead. Yes . . . but no. Breathing is crucial for physical life, but breathing *deeply* is crucial for soul life. I learned to breathe during a diastasis recti recovery program. An odd place to learn to breathe, I know. After having my second child in my thirties, I discovered the dreaded gap between my abdominal muscles. Obviously completely unrelated to this book, but it's my useless piece of personal information for you.

Anyway. Breathing deeply brings oxygen to your brain. It calms your nervous system and allows the blood in your veins to speed around like a toddler after eating their first birthday smash cake. Breathing is powerful enough to override the fight or flight response, connects your mind to your body miraculously, reduces stress, relieves pain, and improves immunity. So, learn how to breathe. Here's one of my favorite breathing exercises if you need a place to start.

— DARKNESS DEEP DIVE #6 —
4-7-8 Breathing Technique

4-7-8 breathing is really straightforward and easy to do throughout your day. Start in a comfortable upright sitting position. Inhale through your nose for a count of four. Hold the inhale for a count of seven. Exhale completely through your mouth for a count of eight. Making a whooshing sound as your exhale helps, even though you look and sound a bit silly.

Repeat this cycle three more times and practice this a few times a day.

THERAPY

Therapists have an amazing wealth of knowledge and a multitude of resources to help you along the way. You're going to need all the help you can get in life—and that is okay. You aren't alone. Therapists care about your mind and want to help you make sense of your emotions. I know that therapy can seem scary. There is a lot of stigma surrounding this subject, but just know that we all need therapy at some point in life. I believe that every single person on this earth would benefit from continued therapy from a young age. Regardless of if you have been through significant trauma, had a hard life or a seemingly easy path—we are all human and we are all imperfect with emotions bigger than we are at times. It is helpful to have a trained individual to help you process through all the things.

Your success in therapy is largely contingent on finding a therapist you're comfortable with. Finding the right therapist for you may take time. Allow the process to happen and take it seriously. Just because a therapist has all the accolades doesn't automatically mean they can help you. Your personality and needs are unique, and your therapist needs to vibe with you to effectively help you through the tough stuff.

It may be helpful to make a list of values that are important to you for your therapist to have. Kind of like if you're setting up a profile on a dating site. If you aren't sure what you are looking for in a therapist, don't worry. You'll discover that as you go. Trust your intuition here—if it doesn't feel right and you don't feel comfortable to open up after a handful of sessions, move on. It's not you, it's them.

AN OPEN MIND

This could be the easiest tool there is. It could also be the most difficult. You don't need to have an end goal in mind for this journey. You don't need to set a timer and accomplish a certain set of actions. All you need to do is open your mind to the possibility of growth and learning. You need to have an appropriate mindset going into this journey. I want you to know a few things here:

1. You are not alone.
2. It is okay to not be okay.

Your mindset will not always be healthy. It is going to have moments of despair and hopelessness. You will want to give up and go back to what is easy for you. Push through, take a deep breath, sleep it off. You've got this.

NOTING

Noting is a form of meditation, but it's one that requires much less from your brain and surroundings. It's a great tool to start with if you're feeling a bit intimidated by meditation or if it just doesn't jive with you.

Noting is fantastic when you're feeling overwhelmed within a certain situation. It's also great to bring reality back when you're in a panic attack or just feeling extra anxious for one reason or another. The idea is that you utilize all five of your senses in the present moment. What do you see? What do you hear? What do you smell? Can you taste anything at the moment? Is there anything touching your body that you can describe?

The great thing about this tool is that you can use it anywhere, at any time, and no one can even tell you're doing it. Simply take note of your surroundings. List what you can see, feel, hear, taste, and smell. Do it in your head, say it out loud, or write it down. Whatever works for you in that particular moment.

Doing this activity forces your brain to live in the present moment and, more specifically, in reality. When you're having a panic attack or spiraling down a hole, your brain, reactions, and emotions are all meshed together, preventing your brain from thinking clearly and acting accordingly. Taking note of real, tangible items surrounding you basically kicks out all the chaos and brings you back to the present moment.

You can amp this tool up by creating a sensory kit for emergency use. Place something in the kit for each of the five senses. Here are some options you may want to include in your sensory kit:

- Hard or sour candy
- A stress ball
- Earbuds for playing music
- Your favorite car freshener
- Dry rice, beans, or pasta
- A book or something to read
- Pictures of people or things that make you happy

Additional Tools I Love:

Self-care

Exercise

Music

Movies

Crisis Hotlines

Fresh Air

Going for a Drive

CHAPTER 5
All about Emotions

"Your intellect may be confused, but
your emotions will never lie to you."

— ROGER EBERT —

TYPES OF EMOTIONS

Generally, our emotions fall into two categories: Superficial
emotions and deep-rooted emotions.

Superficial Emotions

Think of superficial emotions as the emotions that are linked
to one solitary event. Like your little sister borrowing your
favorite cropped T-shirt without asking and then spilling hot
sauce on it. You're feeling frustrated and angry.

These emotions are short-lived and have no attachment
to trauma. Usually one to two emotions total, they aren't
large enough to cause emotional wounding, and if we let
them live out their entire, short life cycle, they come and go
without too much interruption of life.

You respectfully express your emotions to your little sister. She apologizes for not asking to borrow your shirt and subsequently not taking care of it and vows not to do it again. You've honored the emotions and set them free.

Deep-Rooted Emotions

Deep-rooted emotions are emotions that are linked to trauma and have grown large enough to cause emotional wounding. Deep-rooted emotions tend to group together with other emotions to create one giant mess of emotional turmoil. Deep-rooted emotions take longer to process than superficial emotions and may be more difficult to heal from as a result.

> Side note: Superficial emotions can grow to be deep-rooted emotions without the attachment of trauma. This happens a few ways: either when we allow our brains to feed a superficial emotion, giving it life when it normally would have been dead, or when a deep-rooted emotion pulls a superficial emotion into its cohort and convinces your brain that the superficial emotion is linked to the trauma. Emotions and brains can be really sneaky.

By the time you're feeling dead inside, you've probably got several groups of deep-rooted emotions setting up cohorts in your shed of darkness. While most of the emotions we deal with here will be deep rooted, each emotion has its place and purpose. Don't discount the superficial emotions!

EMOTIONS TIED TO MEMORIES

More often than not, you've pushed aside a tough emotion because it is tied to traumatic event or negative memory. It's rare that an emotion deemed "difficult" or "too hard to deal with right now" is just a superficial emotion that has appeared out of nowhere, with no foundation. If you feel as though you have several unfounded emotions, you're going to need to look at them a bit harder. Those "unfounded" emotions are incredibly sneaky, and nine times out of ten actually have a deep-rooted trauma attached to them.

In fact, they can be so sneaky that they build layers upon layers of subsequent memories and emotions between the original traumatic event and the present-day emotion. You can truly become so conditioned to bury the hard stuff that your brain literally does all the work for you without you even realizing it.

It's early evening, mid-summer, and I'm arguing with my boyfriend again. I've said something wrong, and he snapped. He's morphed from his genuine, compassionate, fun-loving self into an unrecognizable monster. The conversation has shifted into unfiltered emotion. An ugliness that can only be described as pure, controlling fear. I've nestled myself into the corner of the room, curled in the fetal position on the hardwood floor. He's hovering over me, screaming obscenities. I feel like an ant, and he feels infinitely tall. Like a daddy longleg spider, backing me into his web. I started off so strong. Speaking my mind. Embracing my inner independent woman. But this man will eat me alive. I can already feel each layer of confidence shriveling away with each insidious insult. Each perfectly aimed stab. If I am to survive, I must be weak. I must agree and relent. Make peace with the devil and beg for forgiveness. I can deal with myself later.

To this day, just a strong, gruff, male voice can cause my insides to bind together, bracing for impact. I'm instantly mentally back on that floor, curled into a ball, awaiting the end. But, unlike years ago, I know better now. I know that that fear is simply an emotion tied to a traumatic memory and that I have the power to acknowledge it as such and release myself from the obligation of reliving that memory. You have the power too.

VALID EMOTIONS AND POINTLESS EMOTIONS

I have seen this scene or something like it more times than I can count:

> A child is throwing a tantrum in a shopping cart after enduring the great injustice of not receiving the toy she wanted. She's obviously distressed. Her parent is embarrassed and frustrated with her inconvenient emotional moment in the pasta aisle of the grocery store. She's impatiently pleading with the child to stop. Exasperated, her mom begins to demand that the child stop screaming and crying. She lets her know that this is a ridiculous display. Sternly demands that she cut it out. The child cries louder, feeling invalidated and misunderstood. She kicks the ground harder. I'm sure you've witnessed a similar scene.

Who is the one in the wrong here? Is the child wrong for being upset about not getting the princess Barbie with the infinite white, glittering dress? Is the adult wrong for wanting the child to be in a state of calm? I'll let you think about that while I talk about the difference between valid emotions and invalid emotions.

For something to be deemed valid, it needs to have a basis of sound reasoning or proof to support it. For an act or emotion to be pointless, the act or emotion needs to have served no purpose: good or bad.

Have you come to a conclusion yet? It's a trick question. Neither the child nor the adult is in the wrong here and, drumroll, there is no such thing as a pointless emotion.

The child and the parent are both feeling valid emotions *simply because they are feeling them.* The child is likely feeling sadness or frustration from the original injustice and then added to that the feeling of being unheard or misunderstood by their parent. While the parent is feeling embarrassed and frustrated that such a big emotion is happening at an inconvenient time, coupled with the feeling of unworthiness and inadequacy as a parent.

Each and every human emotion has its place and purpose in our lives. It's okay to feel every one of them and you are not wrong or abnormal when you do. Notice that I didn't say "if you do" because that's how right these emotions are. Every person on this earth has felt them at some point and will feel them again.

Every. Last. One. Of. Them.

So, stop right now and repeat after me: "It is OKAY to feel whatever I'm feeling."

Say it again.

This will be our mantra from this point forward. Normalize feeling—I promise you won't regret it.

Emotions come hard and fast and are rarely alone. In the heat of the moment, we react solely on the emotions. The child kicks and screams. The adult scolds and hushes. It's a vicious cycle that we can learn to positively manipulate both as children and as adults.

So—we've established that you have all the feelings and that its normal. Now, what do you do with them? The first set of options you have is to shelf them or to feel them. Until now, you've likely just been placing them into the depths of your soul as to not deal with them—hence feeling numb and dead inside. This is what I call shadowing an emotion and it can happen two ways: unconscious shadowing and conscious shadowing.

UNCONSCIOUS SHADOWING

My earliest childhood memory is me, sitting cross-legged on the carpeted living room floor of my childhood home. The room is dark and dingy, and the air is heavy around me. My ears are filled with whale noises escaping from a record player on a table near the front window. My parents lounge weightlessly on the couch nearby: slouched and slinky. Slowly, every so often, they both press a wooden pipe to each of their lips and exhale a cloud of smoke into the damp air. The memory ends.

I grew up loathing marijuana. I vowed never to have a close relationship with a user and to never use myself. I never realized why I had such

a hatred for this until I began exploring my emo-
tional wounds. My brain created a safety net for
me by convincing me that marijuana caused
neglect, loneliness, and insecurity.

There are parts of your mind that operate on a level that we are unaware of. Your brain is an amazing vessel of knowledge and operations. So much so that it automatically thinks, reacts, and acts without you even realizing it's doing so.

Have you ever been driving somewhere and gone into autopilot? You arrive at your destination and don't recall the journey to getting there? That's your unconscious mind at work right there.

Unconscious shadowing happens when your brain has already associated an emotion with an unpleasant event and automatically files that emotion away in an attempt to protect you. Especially when dealing with repressed memories, severely traumatic events, and intense emotions, your brain can and will do this without you even recognizing it's happening.

This process is both amazing and frustrating all at once. Take a moment to thank your brain for working so hard to protect you—it truly is amazing. Have patience with your brain as you navigate this journey. The more you assure your brain that you are strong and capable of taking over, the more it will relax and let you take the reins.

> The more you assure your brain that you are strong and capable of taking over, the more it will relax and let you take the reins.

CONSCIOUS SHADOWING

I felt my life pivot that night. I lay there rigid and half-naked. Frozen in time as I watched the egg-shell popcorn ceiling morph into visions of my shattered innocence. Like when you lay in the grass and stare up at the clouds, willing them into pirate ships and hippos; only the grass is a scratchy red and black plaid comforter and there are no clouds, no sky, no tendrils of hair tickling your forehead from the cool breeze. No, not in this scene. In this scene, there's a girl, a boy, a twin bed, and a destroyed friendship. But hey, at least it wasn't my first time, right? Wrong. So very wrong.

I knew it was wrong, and I didn't have the strength to stop him. With the plethora of unconscious emotional baggage in tow, I embarked on a new path—a new low. I allowed my need for acceptance and my fear of conflict to dictate my actions (or lack thereof).

This event was the catalyst for my downfall. In the aftermath of the rape, I began consciously avoiding my emotions. I felt used, exposed, guilty, dirty, and pointless. These feelings began a domino effect inside my shed of darkness. I began experiencing emotions from my childhood in addition to current emotions and I was utterly overwhelmed.

It seemed as though there was no way out of it all. Like I would surely suffocate under all of these emotions. So, I forced myself to be dead inside—to be numb. I let life happen to me and I stopped feeling altogether. I may have been partially dead inside up until this point, but now I was doing it on purpose.

Conscious shadowing happens when you experience an emotion and then make the conscious choice to file it away. This can be the case for myriad reasons, but I find that this type of shadowing happens most often when you have a lot of spinning plates or after you've been numb and dead inside for a while. Emotional overwhelm makes it difficult to fathom, let alone process the feeling of emotions.

Conscious shadowing has its place in your life. There will be times even after this journey that it is perfectly acceptable to decide to take an emotion and place it into your shed of darkness for a while. The important thing here is for that decision to be informed and purposeful instead of out of fear or overwhelm.

CONSCIOUS EMOTIONAL ACCEPTANCE

We've been over the ways that you can avoid feeling, but what happens when you consciously decide to feel? This is where the magic happens, my friend! When you make the conscious decision to feel your way through an emotion, you're letting your brain know that you are in the driver's seat.

You've got this now. You can navigate through the emotion, explore the reasons why it's affecting you and decide what to do with it. When you take this approach to emotions, your mind and body begin to sync up and eventually a sense of peace and control will surround your thoughts and actions.

By giving yourself the license to be one with your emotions and thoughts and make sense of them, you give yourself a new lease on life.

Before we get too much further into the land of emotions and begin the activities surrounding emotions, I want to talk about emotional boundaries.

EMOTIONAL BOUNDARIES

Whether you are an empath or not, emotional boundaries are a must. Learn how to set them and practice keeping them. This journey is about you, but it can be difficult to not feel guilty when setting boundaries.

When you don't set emotional boundaries, it's doubly hard for your darkness and light to be in sync. Emotionally, you become bogged down by the swirling of your own life events combined with those that surround you. By setting emotional boundaries, your mind has a chance to take a breath and focus in on you. When you set and follow healthy emotional boundaries, you are able to differentiate between yourself and others. As a result, your self-esteem improves, you have a greater sense of identity, and you feel less resentment toward others.

Setting emotional boundaries can look like

- Choosing to stay in when all your friends are going out, because you realize that you have a lot going on in your head.

- Choosing to surround yourself with individuals that have similar energy as yours.
- Removing yourself from a situation that feels like "too much."
- Allowing yourself the freedom to not become emotionally invested in others' life "drama."
- Allowing yourself the grace and freedom to simply *feel*.

Emotional boundaries can be difficult to navigate. You may have friends and family that are offended when you set these boundaries—especially if you haven't been setting them up until this point. That's okay—other people's emotions are not your responsibility. It's okay if they get angry. It's okay for you to say NO. You do not need permission to work on yourself, nor do you need to explain yourself when you decide to spend time alone with your thoughts and emotions. *You* are the most valuable investment you will ever make.

Letting all your friends and family know that you're working on an inner journey for yourself and that you may need to devote more energy on your mind, body, and soul can be helpful. Give them a heads up that you may not be as emotionally available for them right now. Ask for their support as you navigate this journey. Who knows, maybe you'll get a few much-needed cheerleaders.

If setting boundaries is difficult for you, or you're feeling some anxiety at the thought of doing this, here's a helpful activity.

— DARKNESS DEEP DIVE #7 —
Setting Boundaries

Compose an email, letter, or journal entry of what you might say to your network of friends and family regarding this journey and the subsequent boundary you need to set. Take some time to really think about this. You may end up sending this, or it may just serve as a tool to get the thoughts and worries out of your mind. Either outcome is acceptable.

Think about including your reasoning for taking this time to work on yourself (what are your "whys"?), your feelings toward this group of people (how much you appreciate them, etc.), what this journey might look like for you, what you need from them (if anything), and the boundary you need to set. Try to avoid blaming, shaming, or conveying defensiveness in your communication.

Using Darkness Deep DIVE #13: Managing Out-of-Control Feelings on page 112 regarding the outcome of this communication can be incredibly useful here if you're experiencing anxiety over what their reaction may be.

CONTINUE FEELING, OR NOT

Alright—let's head back to the land of emotions . . .

You've embraced your emotion and let it ride its course. Now what? This next step is key to whether you begin a path of healing or a path of obsessive emotional turmoil. In the early stages of thinking and reacting to emotions, your amygdala takes over.

The amygdala is a small, almond-shaped section of the brain that controls your thoughts, emotions, and initial reactions to a stimulus, and you have two of them. They work with memories and emotions.

That one time you wore heels to school and fell smack on your face in the hallway and all the popular, dreamy boys laughed at you? Oh wait, that was me . . . my amygdala remembers. The time your father snapped at you over dinner when he found out you got a D on your math test? Your amygdala remembers. The amygdala not only remembers these experiences, but it also convinces you to make associations based on these experiences. Like getting a bad grade on anything equates to fear and shame. Now wearing heels triggers a fear of embarrassment inside you . . . or me.

Your amygdala has the best of intentions. It only wants to protect you. To send the word out to other parts of the brain that you're in danger and call in the troops. Such a sweet gesture, don't you think? Your amygdala isn't always perfectly aligned with what you need and want, though. It simply reacts to stimuli and pins flags to experiences to be remembered. In order to take control of your emotions and healing, you'll need to let your amygdala know that you are in control. If you don't do this, you risk falling into the rut of obsessive emotional cycling and perpetual numbness.

OBSESSIVE EMOTIONAL CYCLING

When we let an emotion run its course and then continue to allow that emotion to keep occupying a place in our brain and lives, we end up creating a detrimental process of emotional cycling. While emotions and their thought counterparts have a place and should be allowed to exist within us, they don't always need to be resurrected over and over again.

Is your brain perpetuating a cycle of emotional turmoil? Obsessive emotional thoughts can keep you in a state of turmoil longer than you need to be there, but it can be hard to determine when your soul is asking you to let it feel and when it's telling you to move on. Here are a few questions you can ask yourself when you aren't sure:

- Is this emotion serving a worthwhile purpose?
- When did this emotion begin?
- Where is this emotion rooted?
- Has this emotion created a wound that needs healing?

If you answer these questions and you do find yourself in a state of obsessive emotional cycling, it's beneficial to give yourself a bit of a reality check.

— DARKNESS DEEP DIVE #8 —
Releasing Obsessive Emotions

For this activity, let's take an experience that has a strong emotion or set of emotions attached to it. Write that experience down, as well as the emotions surrounding it. Take a look at all of the elements on the page and spend some time deciding if the emotions and thoughts are realistic and if they have a useful place in your mind going forward.

If they are causing you more harm than good, let your amygdala know. Have a conversation with it. Tell it you appreciate it protecting you when you needed it to. Let your amygdala know that you value it. Tell it that when it comes to this situation, you no longer need protecting. That it can lower the flag pinned to this experience. Then imagine taking that flag down. Place it nicely on the ground, burn it, throw it out the window of your mind—whatever suits you.

If you find that your amygdala still tries to remind you of these thoughts and emotions in the future, gently remind it of this deal that you've made.

Ultimately, you get to decide whether you want to continue to allow that emotion to control your body or not. Sometimes you may need to give that emotion some more time inhabiting your being to fully heal. Other times, the best thing to do is to let that emotion die out.

Only you will know what is best for your certain situation and each situation and emotion will likely be different than the last. Listen to your body, speak to your soul, and honor your emotions. They will guide you on the right path to healing.

ALLOWING EMOTIONS TO MARINATE

We need to stop allowing our brains to convince our hearts to stop feeling for fear of feeling incorrectly. Read that again. There is no such thing as feeling incorrectly. There is only *feeling*. It's what we do after the feeling that really matters. Do we examine the feeling and process it? Do we dwell on it and let it overcome our thoughts? Do we ignore it?

We need to stop allowing our brains to convince our hearts to stop feeling for fear of feeling incorrectly.

The best way to honor an emotion is to feel it. It may be scary, and you may be thinking, "But what if I go too far? What if I feel all of my emotions and I never feel happy again?" When you've been shut off from the world of feeling for such a long time, it can be difficult to imagine letting those emotions take over and ever feeling anything good again once you do. They can really pile up in the shed of darkness. I know from experience. Here's a question you should ask yourself—am I really feeling true happiness in life right now?

If the consequence for feeling emotions is never feeling happy again, then you are already living that consequence. You can only go up from here.

When I was nineteen or twenty years old (it feels like a lifetime ago), I began to experience an array of symptoms. Numbness and tingling in my extremities, heart palpitations and chest pain, periods of dizziness, confusion, and lethargy. I went to doctor after doctor who each performed their own tests. I wore heart monitors, underwent MRIs, had extensive bloodwork done—all inconclusive. There was nothing wrong with me. How could I feel all of these things and there not be a medical explanation for any of them? I felt as though I was going crazy.

As a last-ditch effort, I went to see a different kind of doctor—one that took a bit more of a natural approach to medicine. She went over my entire history, both medically and mentally, and finally started asking the right questions. I was diagnosed with severe anxiety and panic attacks.

Even with seemingly no reason for me to feel anxious or stressed, my body was constantly on edge. Every single one of my symptoms was a direct result of a lifetime of unfelt, bottled-up emotions. I was quite literally overflowing with pain.

Our bodies can only house so much hurt before our walls begin to crack. We can only shove so many raw feelings into our sheds of darkness before the foundation begins to crumble under the weight of our lives.

— DARKNESS DEEP DIVE #9 —
Marinating in Emotions

Find a comfortable place to marinate. I use my cabin, but you can use whatever works for you. Start with a few deep breaths. In through the nose, out through the mouth. Relax that jaw—I can feel the tightness from here. Close your eyes.

Imagine that all of your sadness, anger, and insecurities lie at the bottom of your body. If you're lying on your back for this activity, then they have settled along your spine. If you're sitting up, they are nestled just underneath your tail bone. Breathe into that area and picture yourself becoming one with this area and its contents.

Just sit with this awhile. Allow the emotions to come and go as they please. Try not to fight a physical reaction if you have one. If you find tears welling up in your eyes, let them well up. If you find yourself getting too anxious or spiraling, grab a tool. My favorite for this activity is the "noting" tool (see page 79).

Marinate for as long as you feel you need to. You should come out of this activity feeling a bit more connected and in tune with your body as a whole. When you're finished, choose an emotion that stood out to you or still lingers in your mind. Write this emotion down in your notebook for the next activity.

DISSECTING AN EMOTION

In order to get to the root of an emotion, sometimes you have to dissect it and see it for what it really is. When you dissect an emotion, you're searching for understanding, clarity, and guidance from that emotion to bring you closer to healing and blending the darkness and light.

This process is not easy. It's hard, messy, and confusing at best. It means being real with yourself and your past experiences. It means accepting what has happened to you and redirecting blame where it belongs. Dissecting emotions can feel heavy, overwhelming, unbearable, and inescapable. But it can also feel liberating, light, and peaceful. You are going through the process of releasing years of pain and suffering, little by little.

This part can get pretty time consuming depending on how much trauma you have packed away into your darkness. Luckily, you don't need to do this all at once. In fact, I prefer that you don't. You're unpacking a lot of ignored emotions here—it's not meant to happen in one sitting, or even overnight. This is a journey, remember? It's okay if this takes you years to do.

— DARKNESS DEEP DIVE #10 —

Dissecting Emotions

Take that emotion from the previous activity and give it its own page in your notebook. It deserves the singled-out attention after being starved for so long. Begin as always—with a few deep breaths to center yourself. Write down anything that comes to mind when you revisit this emotion. How does this emotion make you feel deep down? Think about where it may have come from originally. Does this emotion affect your daily life? All of these thoughts and insights should go onto the page.

This activity may bring up subsequent emotions that need to be dissected (hence the time-consuming comment). Try not to get disheartened if this happens. Give yourself grace and allow your soul some time to process. You didn't get to feeling dead inside in a day, and you won't get to feeling completely alive in a day either. Jot down any lingering emotions in your notebook and address them when you're ready.

If there are thoughts that come up within this activity that can be solved, solve them. If they need nurturing and acceptance, provide that. If they need to be set free, set them free.

You do not have to repeat the activities for each and every emotion that you unpack from your shed of darkness. For some emotions, it's enough to just unpack them and gain the clarity surrounding them, and then they set themselves free. Other times, you need to be the one to set them free.

CHAPTER 6
The Contributors and the Enablers

I'd like to talk about some common contributors and enablers to feeling disjointed. These could be a reason you began ignoring your darkness or why you continue to ignore your darkness, or even both. This is not an all-encompassing list but rather some common reasons why you may be feeling the way you're feeling.

LEARNING BY EXAMPLE

I've touched on this already but let me reiterate. We begin acting as young adults based on what we were taught as children—both directly and indirectly. We learn from example.

I grew up in a home where tumultuous parental fights, screaming, crying, and emotional manipulation were the norm. My parents, largely due to their own upbringing, did not teach my sisters and me to express our emotions. Our household was not a hugging, emotional, Brady Bunch type of household. We didn't have conversations about how we were doing, how we were feeling, or anything else of the sort. We were taught by example to just keep on trudging through life.

I ignored my darkness for so long as a young adult because of my tumultuous beginning; my subconscious taught my conscious mind that expressing emotions was ugly and unwanted. That all it would do for me would be to make me sad and disappointed in myself. I learned from watching my parents solely express their emotions through arguments and negativity that expressing emotions equaled turmoil and stress. After repeatedly watching the result of those expressions manifest as pain, frustration, and abuse, I naturally wanted nothing to do with expressing emotions.

Maybe you grew up similarly to me, in a household that frequently expressed emotions in a negative way. Maybe you grew up in a household that didn't express emotions at all. Maybe you grew up with extremely positive parents, which, like we explored briefly earlier, can be damaging to the connection with your darkness.

When you grow up with constant positivity, you learn to be positive all the time. This can cause fear and guilt surrounding the expression of any sort of negative emotion. If you learn that all you are supposed to feel is joy, happiness, and love, this may cause you to push aside any feeling that isn't within the parameters of normal for you.

As children, we need to know that whatever we are feeling is okay and normal. We need to be coached through feeling our emotions and either making sense of them or coming to terms with and accepting them. For parents, this is not always an easy task. Many parents are also working from what they learned as children as well as battling the many other factors of life and parenthood.

It's your task, now that you are an adult, to break the cycle and convert any less-than-ideal learned behaviors from your childhood into strengths. To learn from the mistakes our parents or elderly role models may have made and to become the best version of ourselves. This starts with examining your childhood and what behaviors you may have adapted from this era of your life.

Discovering Learned Emotions and Behaviors

Find a comfy place to reflect. Bust out a piece of paper and a pen. Write down a few traits that you recall being prevalent in your household as a child. How did your guardians handle stress? How did they express love? Write down anything that stands out to you regarding the emotional state of your upbringing. Then, in a separate section, write down how you handle emotions now. Do you see any similarities? Put your analytical brain to work here. Put on some Sherlock Holmes in the background if it helps you out. You're looking for clues as to why you are the way you are. Sometimes it even helps to investigate how your guardians were raised—what made them the way they were when you were a child. Make a mental note of what you discover or write it down as well. This can be an incredibly enlightening experience if you are open to the growth.

NATURAL HEALING ABILITIES

Many people have the natural ability to feel another's emotions as their own, or they just have a propensity for wanting to heal another human being. When you are this type of person, you tend to put your own problems and emotions on the back burner. This is a common experience known as empath burnout or emotional burnout.

An empath is someone who experiences the emotions of others.[3] As a human race, we are easily overcome by darkness, evil, and depression. As empaths, or extremely sensitive beings, we feel everything so deeply that it can become difficult to keep the negativity at bay. We must work even harder to filter through our emotions and the emotions of others to get through each day. So, caring for ourselves becomes a monumental task.

Being an extremely sensitive person can be a blessing and a curse. There will always be challenges to having this amazing gift. In the words of Peter Parker's Uncle Ben, "With great power comes great responsibility." Allow it to be your gift. Feeling all the things is an amazing superpower that not a lot of people get to don. You are one of the lucky ones.

If you are an empath, there are many helpful resources available to help you understand your gift, cope with it, and use it to help yourself and others. Podcasts, books, support groups . . . you've got options.

Regardless of your empath status, life is just plain hard sometimes. Since my upbringing was laden with emotional manipulation, my mind convinced my reality that for me to feel and process my emotions meant I was selfish and took energy away from helping others deal with their emotions.

This is a dangerous road to embark upon at any age. It's even more dangerous when you grew up with what some of us refer to as energy vampires. You know the type: the individuals who take and take and never give anything in return. The ones that tend to complain about every aspect of their lives and neglect to see that they have all the power to change what they are unhappy with. These individuals suck the energy out of the natural healers of the world, and we healers just keep listening, investing, and helping.

When a natural healer is raised in this type of environment, they are conditioned to believe that their purpose in life is to fix everyone else's problems. To be there for everyone. To keep the peace and avoid conflict at all costs. At the end of the day, there's no room for their problems, and the healer ends up with some really heavy bricks on their shoulders that aren't even theirs to carry.

— DARKNESS DEEP DIVE #12 —
Managing Outside Emotions and Energies

Begin the day with a clean slate. I like to start my days with a meditation to set my focus and intention for the day. One of my favorites involves imagining a bright, white liquid flowing from above, into my head and filling up all the sections of my body. For me, this creates space and lightness inside my entire being and helps me face the day with patience and gratitude. Carving out the ten minutes each morning to meditate and set your intentions is truly a life-changing act.

Throughout the day, after encountering, helping, or conversing with an emotionally needy person, take a moment and shake out their emotional energy. Seriously—shake it out. Visualize all of the weight of that interaction and all of the emotions that aren't yours flinging from your mind and body like water droplets off of a wet dog as he methodically shakes. Take a few deep breaths—in through the nose, out through the mouth—and return to your day.

End the day with a mental check-in. Find a quiet place to check in with your emotions. Give each one the space to exist freely and then ask yourself if that emotion or energy is yours or someone else's. Be real with yourself. If it's not your emotion, if it's not your energy, set it free. One way to do this is to visualize grasping that emotion and watching yourself toss it out into the world. Watch as it travels further from you, until you can no longer see it. I like to put those emotions in a little mental bubble and watch them float off. You can also send those emotions or energy back to the person they belong with, either by imagining this happen, or by communicating those emotions to the person directly.

Only your emotions are permitted to set up camp inside your mind. We will talk about working through emotions that are yours later on.

NEED FOR CONTROL

I'm a young teenager, sitting quietly in my desk, third row from the front of my fourth-period English class waiting patiently for class to begin. The bell rings, signifying the beginning of our one-hour stint in dissecting To Kill a Mockingbird, *when Trent, the most popular athlete in school, comes nonchalantly stumbling through the classroom door and down my row, recklessly bumping into me before plopping down in the empty seat behind me. Under his breath, but clearly audible, he says, "Watch out, fatty!"*

I was not fat. I was five foot six and 130 pounds. I was beautiful. Yet this simple, disrespectful statement set a fire inside me that would burn for years to come. This statement became the catalyst for my very first control coping mechanism. I couldn't control how others treated me or how my parents treated each other. I couldn't control many things in my life—but I could control my weight. No one would ever call me "fatty" again.

When you're feeling like life keeps handing you obstacle after obstacle and you don't know how to deal with them, it's not abnormal to seek out situations you can control and to become hyperfocused on controlling those situations. We use coping mechanisms because we feel that our entire world—or at least portions of it—is out of control and by clinging to control, we create a safe, predictable environment in which we can survive. We search for avenues that we can directly and immediately control without having to rely on another person. In doing this, we create a false sense of security within ourselves. Consequently, we set ourselves up for a huge letdown when things inevitably spiral out of control. You can learn to relinquish control in some areas of your life while maintaining a healthy amount of control in other areas. Hold tight to your soul when you're feeling out of control. Focus on the healthy things you *can* control and gently let go of all the rest.

— DARKNESS DEEP DIVE #13 —
Managing Out-of-Control Feelings

Start with a short meditation. Guided or not—there's no real wrong answer here. If all you have available to you right now is sitting on your bed and taking a few deep, grounding breaths, I'll take it. The goal here is to get your mind to a calm spot. Feeling cool, calm, and collected? Awesome.

Think of something in your life that feels out of control. It doesn't need to be hugely significant or emotionally charged. Do you feel anxiousness when thinking about natural disasters or a vehicle accident? Does the thought of your child making bad decisions stress you out? Are you about to ride an airplane for the first time, and you're unsure what to expect? Choose one thing and write it down. Now write down all the thoughts you have surrounding this stressor. What do you feel might happen? Why does it feel overwhelming? Why do you want to control it? No answer is too small or "stupid." Anything that comes up is valid.

Some examples using the scenarios from above:

- What if an earthquake hits my town?
- I don't want my child to get hurt.
- I'm nervous I'll embarrass myself.

Take some time to think about each of these. Is there a reason you're thinking or feeling this? Where does it come from?

If you have room next to each of your chosen items, note whether they are controllable or not. **Tip:** you cannot control anyone else's actions or behaviors in a healthy way.

- You cannot prevent an earthquake from happening.
- You cannot control what decisions your child makes.
- You can control your nervousness and thoughts surrounding embarrassment.

The only thing you can truly control is your thoughts. Take your thoughts from this activity and practice replacing them with a positive thought. It's normal to think about bad things happening or to replay a negative event in your life but once you know where the thoughts are coming from and have honored them by processing them, using the genuine power of positivity (as opposed to toxic positivity) is perfectly acceptable and useful. Take the items that you cannot control and practice letting them go or finding a healthy way to help prevent them.

- Do some research on earthquake preparedness. If you have a family, talk to them about what you discover. Come up with a realistic plan if an earthquake does occur. Side note: this does NOT mean that you obsess over coming up with each and every scenario and drill your family for hours to ensure that they have it down to perfection—let me emphasize *healthy* here.

- Lead your child by example. Make smart decisions in your life and use positive reinforcement when your child does make smart decisions. Talk about consequences with your child.
- Find a breathing exercise that helps reduce your anxiousness surrounding this unknown situation. Ask advice from friends and family who have ridden on an airplane so you have an idea of what to expect. Try to give yourself the permission to be human. Humans make mistakes and embarrass themselves from time to time. It will be okay, I promise.

Do this activity as many times and with as many different situations as you need to. The more you practice controlling your thoughts and preventing in healthy ways, The easier it gets. My hope for you is that you'll get to a point where you can stop the cycle of unhealthy controlling right in your mind before it takes control of you.

CORE VALUES

When getting to know your darkness, it's important to recognize the connection between core values and coping mechanisms and ensure that you have a clear vision of your unique core values. Many times, coping mechanisms can be disguised as a core value.

The need to control can be aimed at people or disguised as perfectionism. It also doesn't always look like an obviously unhealthy behavior. For example:

As a teen, I chose an eating disorder as my main coping mechanism in an attempt to feel that I had some semblance of control over my life and what was happening in it. As an adult, I broadened my scope. I became the mom that had planning down to a science. Google Calendar? Yeah, I mastered that. Itineraries? Yup. Making sure to pack ALL. THE. THINGS. Mmmhmmm. I stressed about every little detail. Then, when I did end up forgetting something (because I'm human), I felt like I was the *worst* mom/person in the entire universe. That, my friend, is a coping mechanism hard at work.

The hardest part: as you age, coping mechanisms can become engrained in you. They intertwine with your core values so you can't delineate what is healthy and what isn't. It becomes easy justify your coping mechanisms, accept them as core values, and continue to live under false pretenses.

A core value is something you believe is important in regard to how you live or work. Core values should determine what your priorities in life are. When you align your choices and actions with your core values, it brings contentment to your life. When your core values have become muddled by early emotional trauma, it causes discord and a general feeling of being unsettled.

Here are a few ways trauma survivors justify their coping mechanisms:

Coping Mechanism	Justification or Core Value
Excessively exercising	Taking pride in a healthy body
Running a strict household	Being family oriented
Being a workaholic	Having a strong work ethic and independence
Socially isolating	Identifying as an introvert

Whatever your core values are, this doesn't mean that they are all rooted in trauma—it means that it's *possible* that they are. It also doesn't mean that if they *are* rooted in trauma, that it's a bad thing. It just means that you need to identify what your core values are and where they come from. Once you do that, you can decide if keeping this core value is beneficial to you or if it's contributing to your state of unhappiness.

— DARKNESS DEEP DIVE #14 —

Discovering Core Values

Grab a blank sheet of paper and jot down some of the times in your life that you felt happy, proud, fulfilled, and confident in the choices you were making at that time. Choose some from all aspects of your life (work, school, personal) to ensure you define values that are well-rounded. Answer some questions about each entry:

- Why did you feel what you were feeling? (happy, proud, etc.)
- Were other people involved or did they share in your emotions?
- What desire or goal did you fulfill?
- What other factors were involved in creating this happiness?

Using the emotions from your experiences, select several core values that resonate with you. Here's a list of some of the common core values to help you.

Authenticity	Community
Achievement	Competency
Adventure	Contribution
Authority	Creativity
Autonomy	Curiosity
Balance	Determination
Beauty	Fairness
Boldness	Faith
Compassion	Fame
Challenge	Friendships
Citizenship	Fun

Growth	Poise
Happiness	Popularity
Honesty	Recognition
Humor	Religion
Influence	Reputation
Inner Harmony	Respect
Justice	Responsibility
Kindness	Security
Knowledge	Self-Respect
Leadership	Service
Learning	Spirituality
Love	Success
Loyalty	Status
Meaningful	Teamwork
Work	Thoughtfulness
Openness	Trustworthiness
Optimism	Understanding
Peace	Wealth
Pleasure	Wisdom

Narrow your selections down to your top five core values. If you need help deciding which values are most important to you, try comparing two values and imagining being in a situation where you had to choose which one to honor.

Now, take a look at your top five core values. Make sure they still resonate with you. Do they make you proud? Would you be happy to share your values with others? Would you be willing to stick by these values even when others don't agree? If you answered yes, then we are off and running!

SUPPRESSED TRAUMA

"Birds born in a cage
think flying is an illness."
— ALEJANDRO JODOROWSKI —

I'm about eight years old. I'm securely planted on the top level of me and my younger sister's sturdy, wooden bunk bed. Our bedroom is dark, and my sister is below me softly crying. Even as a young child, I can feel her pain multiple feet away. The tension is palpable. Above everything else, the familiar sounds of our parents screaming envelop me.

I pull my blue-and-white bear blanket up to my neck as if it will deflect the loud noises from permeating my heart, but it seems to increase in intensity and volume. I slam my eyelids shut and begin to sing. Softly at first, then louder. My smallest sister joins me and together we fight against the deafening words.

That memory is one of a handful of memories that my subconscious mind didn't suppress as a result of emotional trauma—just one snippet of my childhood years. I couldn't tell you who won that battle that night. I couldn't tell you what my parents were fighting about. I can tell you that music saved me that night, and it wouldn't be the last time.

It's an odd notion: to think back on my formative years and recall only selected moments. Up until recently, I thought it was completely normal to not remember the bulk of your early years, and one of the most terrifying things that ever happened to me was realizing that I had no idea what my early life was like.

Like some messed up version of childhood amnesia, I had no actual recollection of anything that occurred before I was ten years old. All I had were snippets of a life that I believed were mine. Small clips out of a movie reel that could have even been a dream. None of them seemed real—a scene here, a few moments there, but nothing of substance.

The stunning realization that not remembering my childhood was abnormal created an instant and paralyzing skepticism inside of me. I began to question everything—including myself. No one was safe inside of my mind. This realization didn't come to me until I was in my early thirties, married with a child of my own and two stepchildren. By then, I had lived my entire life in the bliss of ignorance. Never knowing that all my decisions and actions were fueled by a severe longing for love and validation, slung upon a creaky, ambiguous foundation.

There are many times when what is happening to you is too difficult for your brain to process, so, in the interest of surviving, your subconscious will make the executive decision to pack the memories and emotions into the darkness. It's really this amazing gift that our minds give us to protect and nurture us and help us to survive in any given moment.

In my case, my subconscious decided that it was best for childhood-me to tuck those tough emotions and memories into the darkness in order to survive. Sometimes we don't make the conscious choice to hide our trauma. Our subconscious goes into fight-or-flight mode and does what it needs to do to survive.

One of the best things we can give to ourselves in return is to reassure our minds that we are okay now. That whatever happened is in the past. To heal from the emotions and make space in your mind for all of life's possibilities.

You have a few options here. You can dig those memories up, relive them, process them, and heal from them, or you can accept that your memories may always be buried and heal from the emotions anyway.

If you're ready to dive into the realm of reprocessing repressed memories I would highly recommend seeking a professional who can guide you through this process. There are multiple ways to reprocess repressed memories, but they all require you to be incredibly emotionally vulnerable. This can be pretty scary, so it's a good idea to have a professional there to guide and help you. If you would like to accept and heal from the emotions regardless of how much of the memory you have attached to the emotion, a good place to start is to comfort your inner child.

Comforting Your Inner Child

This activity involves getting in touch with your inner child. Letting them know that everything will be okay.

Pick an emotion or memory (if you have even a portion of it) and travel back to that place in your mind. If you don't have a memory tied to the emotion you're working on, that's okay. Imagine your younger self in an empty room, overcome by that emotion. Join yourself in that memory or empty room. It's time to give yourself the comfort and reassurance you needed back then. Give yourself a huge hug. Let yourself know that it's okay to cry—you're there and you won't let them fall. Let yourself know that they are loved and no longer need to hide. That it's okay to feel whatever they're feeling and it's not their fault. Forgive your younger self if you need to.

Watch as that empty room fills up with happiness, joy, and love. Watch as the door to that traumatic memory opens and just outside that door, freedom awaits. Watch as your younger self frees themselves from the burden of the traumatic emotion. Take a deep breath and come back to reality.

The first opportunity I had to do this activity was truly life changing for me. I chose the memory that I shared with you earlier. I watched as the scene unfolded. I felt each and every emotion in my adult body, but this time I emerged from my corner and walked over to my childhood bed. With tears in my eyes, I ascended the ladder and joined myself on the bed. I snuggled into the blankets with her and engulfed her in my arms. I felt the tension in her body release as she melted into my embrace. Together, we took a giant inhale and exhaled all the uncertainty of the day. I whispered into her ear, "You are strong, you are okay, and you are loved." I watched her face intently as one final tear trailed down her cheek and she softly closed her eyes and fell asleep.

STRIVING FOR PERFECTION

> "Perfection is a road,
> not a destination."
>
> — UNKNOWN —

As humans we are bombarded with ideations of perfection. We are pushed to have the best of everything—the prettiest face, the most put-together family, the nicest car, the highest paying job, the fittest body. As a result of this conditioning, many people hide and ignore their darkness in order to maintain the allure of perfection.

On a daily basis, we consume constant criticism from social media about our bodies: how thick or thin our thighs are, the circumference of our biceps, the shape and size of the features on our faces, even our skin color.

In March of 2019, The Mental Health Foundation and YouGov conducted a series of online surveys regarding body image.[4] The results showed that

- 20% of adults felt shame, just over 34% felt down or low, and 19% felt disgusted because of their body image in the last year.
- Among teenagers, 37% felt upset and 31% felt ashamed in relation to their body image.
- 34% of adults said they had ever felt anxious or depressed, 35% of them because of their body image.
- 13% of adults experienced suicidal thoughts or feelings because of concerns about their body image.
- 21% of adults said images used in advertising had caused them to worry about their body image.
- 22% of adults and 40% of teenagers said images on social media caused them to worry about their body image.

We are also frequently engulfed in mass media opinions about the "right" way of life, the proper way to act and speak, even the popular way to think.

After a while, this societal pressure weighs down our souls and hardens our hearts. When we hang on to this idea of perfection, we begin to become an unrecognizable version of ourselves. We become so bogged down with others' view of humanity that it's difficult to see our true selves anymore.

We begin to absorb our surroundings and start to hide anything about ourselves that isn't up to the "standard." What's worse is that at some point, a lot of people believe that this new version of themselves is the authentic version. It can be incredibly confusing. It can be even more difficult to realize and come to terms with the fact that it isn't. Because underneath all the insecurities and masks we put on lies the person you are meant to be. Perfectly flawed and authentic.

— DARKNESS DEEP DIVE #16 —
Working through Perfectionism

Think back to when you were a child—I know, I ask that of you a lot. Think of a time when you were blissfully happy. Maybe it's a memory of playing make-believe with your siblings. Or cuddled up in bed reading a book. Your memory might be of a time in your teens camping with your close friends. Whatever your memory is, take a minute to examine it. Were you concerned with the way you looked while you were playing Barbies? Were your thoughts consumed with the idea that someone might be able to tell that you purchased the jeans you're wearing on clearance? The likely answer is "no." As children, most of our brains are so pure and unburdened with negativity that we simply exist. We need to get back to simply existing more often.

Think about how you feel about those things now. Are there things in your life that you strive for perfection in? Does the journey to gaining that perfection bring you joy or stress? Do you feel good enough?

Capture the emotions surrounding the answers to these questions and imagine what will happen when you give yourself grace in achieving perfection. When you accept that perfection is truly unattainable. Most of us have at least a few unrealistic and unhealthy expectations for ourselves. I want you to take moment and write down at least one expectation that you have for yourself that is unrealistic or causes you negative stress. List some reasons why this expectation is unattainable and how it affects you and your life. Then list some ways that you can ease up on this expectation. That could mean working to remove the expectation completely or shifting the expectation so that it isn't as harsh. You could list some alternative expectations that are realistically attainable. List some ways that you can better yourself in this area that don't cause you stress.

As you move through your daily life, remind yourself of the negative repercussions of carrying extreme expectations for yourself. Practice telling yourself that you are enough, just the way you are. You could even place notes on a mirror or other highly visible place to remind you what you want to strive for. Positive affirmations do have their place in your life—you don't need to delve into your darkness all the time.

FEAR OF CHANGE

Humans like safety because we can count on it. We can wake up and plan on not being hurt that day. We can head out the door in the morning and know exactly what to expect at work, school, or home. It's comforting to not have the anxiety of any single day hanging over your head. Because of this, it's natural for your subconscious to dislike change—good or bad.

You are currently residing in this controllable place where you can be "perfect": a safety net that allows for steady forward movement in time. The problem with the safety net is that it's a net. Like a fish caught in a fisherman's net, you're trapped there without any possibility of exploring that lake or ocean. You'll likely be left gasping for air as that net is dragged through the water out of your control.

The net may be safe and surefire, but the net isn't necessarily good for you. Removing that safety net is scary. You risk judgment, failure, and even being eaten up by that big, ugly shark.

Your subconscious can't determine whether any given change will be a positive experience or a negative one on its own. You need to reassure your subconscious that the change is okay. Your subconscious thrives on consistency because it's safe, obviously. Even if the consistency is causing a negative effect on your soul and life. It's predictable; therefore it removes the possibility of a surprise fight-or-flight reaction.

Your darkness is built for change. It's always ready to take on surprise emotions. It will guide you through that soul-searching journey if you let it. Let it be your partner as you venture into the ocean, and eventually that darkness will become your safety net. The one place that you can go to express yourself limitlessly.

Before you begin to embark upon change, you'll need to learn to reassure your mind that what you're going through will be good for you in the long run. That it's okay to endure some pain while you fight for clarity, happiness, and creativity.

— DARKNESS DEEP DIVE #17 —

Embracing Change

Choose a situation that involves a big change in your life or your mindset. Maybe it's this journey that you are on right now. Write it down in your notebook. Let's explore the pros and cons of the change.

- How could the change negatively affect your life?
- How could it positively affect your life?
- What challenges might you face during this period of change?
- What is the worst that could happen?
- What is the best that could happen?

Just the simple act of thinking through the process of change prepares your brain for acceptance and forward movement. Writing it down creates a space of comfort within your mind, eliminating doubt and insecurity. It's okay to feel whatever you're feeling in this moment of change. Reassure yourself that you can conquer anything. You are strong, and embracing this journey will lead you to yourself.

NO TIME TO FEEL

You just have too much on your plate to deal with pesky things, like feeling deeply. Yep—that's a sad reality. We are just too busy to deal with our emotions, so we push them aside.

As children, it's much easier to allow each emotion to take over for a period of time. We don't have families to raise, dinner to prepare, financial worries or any of the other things that adulting brings to our life (for better or for worse). We have all the time in the world to lay on the ground flailing our arms and legs while tears stream uncontrollably down our cheeks. We can scream at the top of our lungs in apparent agony because we just didn't want the broccoli on our plate that evening.

As adults, we believe that to indulge in the petty task of feeling deeply and expressing those feelings would mean a distraction from our busy days. One that we just cannot afford to have. We keep this up because, hey, it worked! We shove that frustration with our spouse under the proverbial rug and shower it off—we just couldn't bear the thought of communicating it and having it turn into a full-fledged discussion when we still had a kitchen to clean and kids to tuck in.

We decide that to express our disappointment with not getting that promotion at work would derail our path to success for the next promotion, so we hold it inside.

We do this thinking it is what is best for us. That we should keep pushing through the negative emotions and focus on our tasks and goals. The reality is that by pushing all of those emotions into the darkness, we are blocking the outlet for our light.

We are temporarily relieving stress from our immediate situation and instead placing the overwhelm onto our inner self. The result is far from what we intended. What ends up happening is everlasting overwhelm, a feeling that you're never enough, creative blocks, confusion, and self-doubt. If we can learn to feel each emotion as it comes, let it fully develop, process it, and then move on, we would free up so much space in our soul for authentic light.

How do you make time to feel when you have so much going on? I get it—you have a lot of spinning plates. I know what you're thinking: how in the hell am I going to carve out time to deal with my emotions when I can barely carve out time to eat? If it seems impossible, that's okay. In fact, it's normal. I'm not telling you that you should spend hours each day mulling over the day's emotions. Small, attainable goals are key. Here's what I'm asking: just *try*.

— DARKNESS DEEP DIVE #18 —
Making Time to Feel

Start with processing your simpler emotions— the ones that don't feel like they're tied to a core value or traumatic event. Choose a goal that feels attainable to you. Can you focus on processing three superficial emotions each day? The great thing about superficial emotions is that if we let them run their course, they don't last long. The next time you experience a superficial emotion, let yourself feel it. Marinate in it. If you need to address the emotion with another person and feel that you can do that productively, do it! Then tell your brain to stand down. There's no need to dwell on that emotion. Take a deep breath and with the exhale, imagine that emotion escaping your body through your breath, and disintegrating into a billion microscopic fragments in the air.

As you begin this emotion-processing journey, it may take some time to convince your brain to stop the obsessive emotional cycle. Our brains tend to resist change when they believe they are thinking out of protection. It's okay if it takes some time. Be patient with your brain as it's learning new coping mechanisms. You may need to repeat the breathing exercise multiple times over a period of time for a single emotion. You can even try imagining an alternate, positive emotion entering your body on the inhale if you want to get crazy.

PHASE 2 REFLECTION

*What new tools have you added to
your toolbelt after this phase?*

*What healthy and unhealthy boundaries
to you have? Do you find it difficult to
assert new healthy boundaries?*

*How did you feel after marinating in and
dissecting your emotions? Did you notice
any shifts in your mindset or mood?*

*Are you holding on to anything that
contributes to or enables numbness? Why?*

*Do you think that your current actions
align with your ideal core values?*

How will you make time to feel?

PHASE 3

Vital Creativity

Phase three is all about seeing the
payoff of all the work you just put in.
It's about giving your darkness
a healthy outlet.

Let's deep DIVE into creativity.

CHAPTER 7
Creative Healing

So, what if you could take that darkness—all the sadness, the fear, the negativity—and harness it into something great? Something that enhances who you are instead of stifles it? Something that helps your soul grow and change with ease? Something that inspires others to create, to be authentic, and to live life to its fullest? Spoiler—you can!

Now that you've come this far, I can let you in on the secret. Embracing your darkness is the first step to unleashing your creative beast and the two go hand in hand. As you are deep diving into the depths of your sadness and misery, having creativity with you gives the emotions an outlet. A way to communicate when communicating seems too difficult.

Creativity was my companion. It urged me; it spoke for me when I couldn't speak. It listened when I didn't even know I was talking. It was there for me when I had no one. It *was* me when I didn't know who I was. Let creativity guide you through the adventures of solitude and grief. Let it be your life raft when you're drowning. It can pull you to safety.

You may have already experienced this divine gift. Either prior to embarking on this journey, or even during this journey. Have you ever felt strangely driven to create during a bout of anger, depression, or anxiety? Maybe you didn't recognize the secret ingredient for what it was.

DEFINING CREATIVE HEALING

> "Invention, it must be humbly admitted, does not consist in creating out of void, but out of chaos; the materials must, in the first place be afforded: it can give form to dark shapeless substances but cannot bring into being the substance itself."
>
> — MARY SHELLEY, *FRANKENSTEIN* —

So, let's talk about being creative. Creativity is defined as "the use of the imagination or original ideas, especially in the production of an artistic work."[5]

When the word *creativity* is used, many people automatically associate creativity with artistic talent, and, while that may be true in many cases, it is not always the case. Creativity means being open to possibilities and change.

Creativity is not a one-size-fits-all type of deal. It can come in a multitude of forms. For me, creativity comes in the form of writing, crafting, and interior design. For others, it may be painting, drawing, or making music. Some non-artistic ways of creating could be playing a game of chess, learning a new language, sewing, coding, or creating a s'mores bar with options and variations to the classic s'more and inviting your friends over to partake. (I'd totally show up to that.)

What I'd like to emphasize here is the section of the definition that tells you that creativity is simply the use of your imagination. As children, we are constantly creating. We create fantastical stories at the drop of a hat, we create Lego fortresses and entire dimensions of reality in less than a day. Children can so easily access their creativity, and as adults, we encourage that process in them. We purchase them toys that enable worlds to be built and characters to come to life. We provide paper and crayons so that a scene may spark to life.

> Creativity is simply the use of your imagination.

We have so little to worry about as children most of the time that our brains are free to explore the realms of creation. As we grow older and become plagued with the obstacles life hands us, we tend to focus less on creating and more on surviving. Our imagination shifts from imagining positive things to imagining negative things. We worry about what will happen in the future, and all the "what-ifs" of life and shove our creative imaginations aside. We learn that real life is more important than make-believe. Our creativity is buried underneath the piles of baggage shoved into our shed of darkness. When you tap into that creativity, one thing it can help with is your healing process.

THE BENEFITS

Creating is so vital for your emotional, mental, and physical well-being. When you create, a section inside your soul opens up. You are more able to process emotions and react appropriately. Creating allows for a nonverbal outlet in which to make sense of and express your emotions, and science agrees.

Multiple studies have shown that art helps people express emotions that are too difficult to put into words. Expressive writing helps individuals overcome trauma and increases memory and the ability to learn. Those with musical training have improved connectivity between the hemispheres of their brain. Individuals that participated in theater performances had improved psychological well-being and better cognitive functioning after four weeks. Writing helped HIV patients boost their immune systems and has been known to help with chronic pain management. Dancing helps with positive body image.[6] The benefits are endless!

Create! Even if for you that means creating journal entries or cooking a meal. Create a world in Minecraft. Color a stick-figure picture on lined paper. Imagine an alternate universe. It doesn't have to be a huge endeavor and you do not have to be good at it! The only requirement that creativity has is that you enjoy it. That's all.

Create when you're sad, create when you're mad, create when you're anxious. Find your niche and allow creativity to filter the baggage out of your shed of darkness.

WHAT CREATIVE HEALING LOOKS LIKE

I was a teenager when I met him. My first "love" and the boy who introduced me to the thing that ultimately saved my life. He entered my life in the form of a fuzzy-haired guitar player, a friend of a friend, and he was infectious. His energy and wit emanated, and without any effort on his part, his sense of humor lightened the heaviness that existed within my soul. The harshness of the world disappeared when I was with him.

He was musical on so many levels and, as such, he came with a library of melodies. Now my newest addiction. Without even thinking, I fell hard. My brain settled the instant the music flooded my eardrums. It wasn't the music alone. The words that accompanied the noise were like a long-lost friend. Something inside me clicked into place that time. A chunk of my soul was found in the creative outbursts of others. He introduced me to band after band. My collection grew. My soul emerged. Still now, the beauty in finding yourself in a stranger's soul will never cease to floor me.

He was the typical band-boy. He had an on-again, off-again girlfriend in his hometown an hour away. I was the other girl, and he was a man to adore, to fight for attention, to long for. To break my heart—and break my heart he did. Countless tears were shed over him. Each one staining the page of my newest outlet. Poetry.

The colossal damage inflicted upon me left me no choice. My insides were writhing once again. Performing somersaults within each vein, each organ. Begging for release once more. My fingers reached for the tool to communicate. My emotions fighting their way to the surface. The strokes began and didn't stop this time. Only, instead of a sharp object to express, my hands chose a pen. My scribbles turned to words, to broken sentences, to partial lines, to paragraphs. My first poem was born. My soul was reborn.

September, 2002

*Your unintended persuasion causes me to fall.
I let myself go, I slipped into your heart and soul.
Falling eternally through the never-ending
twists and turns of your brain.
Never until now did I realize how
incredibly complex this is.
The unspoken words tear me apart inside.
I'm only torn, I can be mended.
But your unheard voice contributes to the tear.
I'm still surviving. My body, my heart, my soul,
are teetering on broken.
Internally I sense the gears in your brain
turning the opposite way.
I fight my hardest to dismiss these feelings,
But the time bears down on my fragile being.
One more day, one more hour,
one minute, one second.
The negative reinforcement of a mechanical
device determines my every happiness.
The stinging of the wound you caused
breaks me down.
Until I'm underneath the earth,
pounding on the ceiling for aid.
I have failed to make myself heard,*

*Or the ears of others have selectively
shut my cries out.
Out of earshot, out of sight, out of mind.
With the exception of you.*

This is a perfect example of how human relationships don't actually shape who you are. It's the emotion. The turmoil. The deep, dark, depths of depression that resulted from that intense connection that shaped who I am. That was the first time that darkness turned to light for me. It wasn't the relationship itself. It wasn't him changing me. It was the connection and the bond that my soul felt with his energy that changed me. It was music and writing that changed me.

When that was ripped from my grasp, I was shattered. That feeling of nothingness and everything all at once. That notion that my chest would undoubtedly collapse if a single more ounce was placed upon it. It was all of this, paired with a perfect melody, that allowed my soul to finally speak.

Without these emotions, creativity cannot be born. And without creativity, your authentic self ceases to be seen, felt, and lived. Your soul needs creativity to flourish and to truly shine.

From that day forward, creating would come in the form of urgent napkin poems. My word vomit. When I'm feeling an emotion particularly strongly, I shove some earbuds in, crank up my angsty vibes, and grab my favorite weapon—a pen. Not just any pen will do, though. It has to be a rather large ballpoint pen. None of this gel, fountain, or liquid crap. I need to feel the paper glide underneath the weight of everything I'm feeling. Ballpoint does this for me.

Once I have my weapon and my spectator (the paper) I just let it go. Whatever is inside of me—I let it out. Sometimes it makes no sense—it's gibberish and insane. Sometimes it's a letter. Other times it's an insanely beautiful alliteration of the emotions running rampant inside of me.

There are times when I'm word vomiting holed up in a closet with tears streaming down my face. Other times I'm pretending to write an email to a client. Over the years I've perfected my word vomiting skills. Sometimes I don't even need the music (though it's always better with it).

The point is, I've learned to use my creativity as an outlet. I've trained myself to use it when I need it and pack it away when it isn't appropriate because a lot of the time, my creativity comes in the form of a certain darkness. And that's okay. That darkness is what allows my light to shine even brighter. Find your darkness and give it creativity.

If creativity is foreign or scary to you, here are a few fun options to open your mind up and get the creative juices flowing.

Prompting Creativity

- Grab a piece of paper and a helper. Have your helper draw three random lines on the page. The lines can be straight or curved, connected or not. Once you have the lines drawn, create a picture utilizing all three lines. You could create one thing, multiple things, or a scene of some sort. Just create whatever comes to you. Let your mind run with it.

- Grab a dictionary, open it up, and select a word at random. Use this word, the word before it and the word after it to write a short story. If you don't have a dictionary, you could use any book and just select any three random words. It doesn't have to be a serious story—have fun with it!

- Think of your favorite song or a song you listen to when you're sad. Write down the lyrics to this song. Now, try adding a verse to the song.

- Make a list of childhood dreams you had. Which ones have you pursued? Why did you pursue those dreams? Why haven't you pursued the others?

- Take a piece of paper and a pen. Set a timer for one minute, close your eyes and start drawing on the paper. Let your hand go wherever it feels like going. At the end of the minute, open your eyes and look at your drawing (it's going to look ridiculous). What do you see in it? What does it look like to you? Give it a name and write that name at the top of the page.

WHY NOT JUST CREATE?

You may be thinking, *If creativity is so great and healing, why do I need to process emotions? Why not just create them all away?* I told myself that very same thing for a long time. Once I found writing, I threw myself into it. I used it to get the emotions out of me. But it wasn't enough on its own. I needed to process those emotions and make sense of them. Without doing that, I was just using writing as a Band-Aid and never actually healing the wounds. Writing adopted a negative, dark aura. I could only summon my creative talent when I was depressed.

Healing the emotional wounds from your trauma is imperative, but you don't have to heal all of them before you begin creating. They can coexist, and they should. Just like you need darkness and light to express authentically, you need the darkness and the light to create authentically.

Now that you have the foundation and tools you need to process and heal, you can lean on creativity to help you process, express, and heal. You can also lean on creativity to help you find your purpose in life.

CHAPTER 8
Creative Purpose

Believe it or not, everyone is capable of being creative. For some of us, it takes a bit more work to find what we are creative in. When you go through a traumatic experience, your focus is on survival. Your mind isn't given the opportunity to explore creative avenues. Unleashing your creativity is even more difficult when your darkness and light are disconnected from one another. Now that you know how to begin reconnecting them, you have to opportunity to use your creative healing to find your creative purpose.

BUT . . . WHAT'S THE DIFFERENCE?

There are many ways that creative healing and creative purpose intertwine. The main difference between the two lies within your state of mind. Creative healing happens when you use your creativity to help you express your darkness— it's almost as if it comes from a place of panic and desperation. Creative purpose happens when you can clearly look at your passions and creativity and use it to make your life more fulfilling and meaningful.

It's important to keep in mind that just because you've learned how to achieve creative purpose, it doesn't erase the need for creative healing. Sometimes you'll use them in tandem without even thinking about it, and other times you'll use each one on its own. The more in tune you become with your emotions and needs throughout your process, the more you'll recognize when you need to utilize creative healing and when to pay attention to your creative purpose.

Here are a few ways to use each:

Creative Healing	Creative Purpose
Any time an emotional wound needs to heal	To enhance the lives of yourself and others
When you are having difficulty processing an emotion	To maintain emotional stability long term
When you feel trapped inside a traumatic memory	To consistently support creative healing
When you need help moving through a new traumatic event	When you are searching for fulfillment and purpose

It took me many years to filter through my traumatic experiences, realize the difference between relying on my creativity as an outlet and utilizing my creativity to foster a more authentic life. Once I held that clear definition in my heart, I went from writing in a fit of panic and depression to writing for joy and purpose. Writing dark and twisty poetry to writing short stories and novels. In my quest to create, I also found pleasure in woodworking, crafting, hand lettering, and interior design. All of which have offered me peace, stability, and a sense of accomplishment.

Each one has also offered the possibility of new business adventures, new ways to share my talents with the world, and new ways to express my true self. By trusting in my intuition and following my passion, I'm now living through my authentic, creative purpose.

I know that it can feel overwhelming—especially when you've just trudged through a lot of emotional healing. Take your time—there's no rush here. Don't allow the end goal to intimidate you. Start with passion and let it lead you. Enjoy the process!

START WITH PASSION

Passion is the air that creativity breathes and the cornerstone of life—without it, life lacks true meaning and depth, and creativity cannot authentically exist. So, my first advice in finding your creativity is to start with passion!

Finding Passion

Think about all the things that make you happy. The subjects that pull at you, that you can't seem to get out of your head. Are there endeavors you think about pursuing? Things that you think you might like to learn more about or hobbies that interest you? Write a list of items that you think may be a source of passion for you. Choose a few that call to you the loudest and write all the reasons you haven't explored this passion yet.

Once you have your reasons down, see if you can find ways to solve whatever is holding you back. If it's a lack of money, make a goal to save the money. If it's a lack of education, how can you learn the skills needed to pursue this passion? Some of your passions may take time to accomplish—that's okay. The journey is sometimes enough to give you clarity about whether or not this passion truly belongs in your life. Some passions will be easy to explore. If you have several passions that will take a while to explore, I recommend choosing at least one easily attainable passion to go along with it. I want you to be able to see and feel the forward movement.

Here are some tips to help foster the discovery of your passion:

- Don't let fear stop you. Fear can be an incredibly powerful roadblock if you don't know how to overcome it. Luckily, you do! Use the tools you've learned here to reassure yourself and heal from fear. Using fear to hold us back can be a coping mechanism put in place thanks to your past experiences. If that's the case, work through that experience and forge ahead with confidence!

- Don't think too hard. Let the process just happen. When you think too hard about something (especially creativity and passion), it tends to stifle it more. It's the curse of creativity, I think.

- Experiment with a lot of different things. Even things you don't think you'll enjoy. You never know where your passion may live.

- Move on. If something doesn't feel like it sets your soul on fire, move on. That is not to say that you should move on if something is difficult. There are times when I'm writing, and I hate everything that lands on the page—it happens, and it doesn't mean that it isn't meant to be your passion or your purpose. If you feel the fire, stick with it.

- Take note. When you come across things in your day-to-day life that interest you or an idea that you feel fiery about, take note of it. Add it to your list of possible passions and find a way to explore it.

- Make it about you. Your passion and purpose don't require the approval of anyone but yourself. If you feel you should explore a passion, explore it. Don't let the fear and doubt of others get in your way.

- Have fun. As I mentioned earlier, when I was writing solely as an outlet, it became my coping mechanism instead of my creative outlet. If you're not having fun, you need to adjust something.

Once you begin the process of discovering passions and purpose, it's important to remember that your purpose is a road, not a destination. Allow me to explain further . . .

PURPOSE IS A ROAD, NOT A DESTINATION

As humans, we are conditioned to be afraid of failure. We are highly skilled at avoiding the pain that failure brings by never even trying in the first place. This fear blocks vulnerability and creativity, therefore blocking us from finding our purpose. I find it useful to think of purpose as a road, not a destination. Meaning that you will never truly arrive at "purpose." You'll never actually wrap it up into a package and send it off to its next destination. You don't achieve it and then move on to the next thing. You will constantly be traveling down the road to your purpose. When you find it, purpose will join you on the road.

Your purpose may shift as you progress through life, and you may find yourself searching for a new purpose. Continue on that road, my friend. That's the purpose of your purpose—to progress, shift, grow, and adapt. This adaptation is part of what makes you complete.

Summoning the courage to create and live through your passions doesn't require perfection or completion. It requires forward movement and the willingness to be open.

PURPOSE IS WHAT FEELS IMPORTANT

I want to reinforce a point I made early on in this journey. That is your purpose in life is NOT one big, all-encompassing, higher life power. It doesn't only occur once in a lifetime when it's 3:33 a.m. during a full moon. Stop putting so much pressure on yourself—this is supposed to make you feel good, right? Right!

Your purpose in life is all about what feels important to you. What sets your soul on fire. There are always exceptions to this. There will be people that you know, or people that you hear of that, at a young age, know *exactly* what they are meant to do with their life. They graduate early, go on to an Ivy League college and save children in underprivileged countries with their innovative, genius invention. Those people are exceptions to the rule, and while I am so incredibly happy for them and all the children they've saved, quite frankly, they make finding purpose in life a hell of a lot harder for people like us.

I'm in my thirties and still have doubts as to what my purpose in life is. I mean, I know deep down what it is, but I have moments where I think, "Ummm, am I *sure* that's what I'm meant to do? Because it feels really hard right now and maybe I'm meant to do something else . . . "

It's totally normal to have doubts. To question your choices and to feel like straying from your path. Those others are the abnormal ones! Remember that if it's important to you, then it's right. If it gives your life meaning and happiness, keep going. Don't compare yourself to others or size up your purpose versus theirs. We are not all created equally when it comes to purpose.

As long as you are staying true to yourself and showing up authentically, you've succeeded. Keep traveling that road of healing, passion, creativity, and purpose, friend.

PHASE 3 REFLECTION

*Are you currently honoring creativity
in your life? Why or why not?*

What are some things you are interested in?

Are you afraid to fail? Why or why not?

What passion are you going to explore?

PHASE 4

Embrace
and Explore

The final phase is really just the beginning.
This is the part where you live your life!
All you need to do is embrace, explore,
and deep DIVE into the new you.

NOW WHAT?

"Life is a circle. The end of one journey
is the beginning of the next."

— JOSEPH M. MARSHALL III —

Whew! You've made it to the end of this journey with me. Within these pages, I truly hope you've begun to find yourself and give your emotions a voice. It is absolutely critical to your future and the future of our society to begin restructuring our relationship with trauma and our emotions. So, now what?

Moving forward, I hope you'll continue to utilize these activities. Continue to feel and continue to connect with your darkness. As you continue on your path to finding yourself and leaning into your purpose, I want you to remember some things:

Your trauma is valid, your trauma is valid, your trauma is valid. It doesn't matter what anyone thinks of it, how large it is deemed, or how it's classified. If it affected you, it matters!

Continue to make an effort to calm your fight-or-flight reaction. You are in control of your emotions, and you are completely capable of captaining your life!

Be confident! Own your life and experiences. Embrace your journey and don't let anyone tell you you're wrong for feeling.

Don't fear your darkness. It truly is a beautiful part of you.

Use your tools. These are crucial for your success and progress. You wouldn't head to work as a carpenter without the tools needed to complete your job, so don't show up to heal without your mental tools. Also, get new tools—there are a plethora of them out there, and you can never have too many.

Utilize the Darkness Deep DIVEs as many times as you need to. There is no shame in doing this. I've created a quick list for you at the end of the book so you can easily reference them.

Don't forget to adapt and evaluate as you move along. This is not a one-time fix type of deal. You will learn, grow, and change through this journey. Periodically ask yourself if the emotional boundaries you have in place are still valid and healthy. Are you doing everything you can to thrive in each moment and collectively? Keep your reality in check and make sure you're always assessing your core values to ensure that they still align with your authentic self and your reality.

Keep working through those emotions. The more you do it, the better you'll get at it and the easier it will become. Take it slow and steady. There is no one more worth it than you.

Don't forget to breathe, and take in each moment, the positive and the negative. Love yourself. Forgive yourself. And let your darkness shine—you deserve it, friend.

From the bottom of my heart,
thank you for trusting in me.
Thank you for trusting in yourself.
Thank you for feeling.

ACKNOWLEDGMENTS

This book has been nearly a lifetime in the making. As such, many people have contributed to my breakdown, my growth, and my healing. I am grateful for each and every one of you for your unique role in my life.

Kaytleigh, my poodle, you quite literally saved my life. You have transformed me both physically and emotionally. You continue to challenge and amaze me daily. Thank you for being the best, most important thing that ever happened to me. Amelia, you are proof that the universe has a plan for me. Thank you for encouraging me with your pure light and reminding me to enjoy each and every moment of this life. Ben and Aislinn, thank you for embracing me fully and letting me give you bull hugs. I thank the universe every day that you came into my world. Kris, words could never express the gratitude I have for you. Thank you for accepting my journey with an open mind and heart. Without your support, I'd be lost in my darkness. Kelly, thank you endlessly for believing in me. You will forever be my safe place—my person—home. Jill, thank you growing up with me, for being my constant, my adventure buddy, and my bestie. I cherish all of the memories we share. Lucy, without your soul, getting through the hard times would have been a lot harder. Rae, you were the first person to truly accept me for who I am, and for that, you will always hold a special place in my soul. Your acceptance was the catalyst to my healing—thank you from the bottom of my heart. Shaw, thanks for breaking my heart so I could learn how to feel. Mom and Dad, thank you for loving me. For being brave and doing your best. For supporting me in all of my crazy endeavors. I love you both. My sisters, Cari and Brooke, thank you for being my best friends, my support system, my extra clothing, my party crew, and everything in between. I couldn't have asked for better siblings. I love you both end-lessly. Randy, thank you for letting me tag along on your dates, protecting me, and loving me. I wouldn't be who I am without your support.

Thank you to my beta readers and editors: Emily Chambers, Rachael Tanner, Jon Voigt, Catherine Christensen, Justin Greer, Deborah Spencer, and Kaitlin Barwick for offering your opinions and polishing my words when I was tired of looking at them.

This book would not exist without the coaching of Azul Terronez and the gentle soul tugging of Steve Vannoy. I will forever be grateful for the incredible opportunity that fate gave me that October day.

DARKNESS DEEP DIVE
LOCATIONS

REFERENCES

1. "Fight or Flight Response," *Psychology Tools*, https://www.psychology tools.com/resource/fight-or-flight-response.
2. Chapman, Benjamin P et al. "Emotion suppression and mortality risk over a 12-year follow-up." *Journal of psychosomatic research* vol. 75,4 (2013): 381–5. doi:10.1016/j.jpsychores.2013.07.014.
3. *Merriam-Webster's Online Dictionary*, s.v. "empath," https://www .merriam-webster.com/dictionary/empath.
4. "Body Image Report—Executive Summary," *Mental Health Foundation*, https://www.mentalhealth.org.uk/publications/body-image-report/exec -summary.
5. *Lexico*, s.v. "creativity," https://www.lexico.com/en/definition/creativity.
6. Maria Cohut, "What Are the Health Benefits of Being Creative?" *Medical News Today*, February 16, 2018, https://www.medicalnews today.com/articles/320947.

ABOUT THE AUTHOR

E. K. RICHARDS is a creative junkie, dog lover, and connoisseur of emotions. She began her journey through life in sunny Southern California, where she established a deep love of the ocean and a small obsession with mermaids. Most of her life, however, was spent growing up in Utah, nestled up against the Wasatch mountains.

Richards has always had a strong interest in psychology and the inner workings of the human mind. As such, she studied psychology and social work at Utah Valley University and is a proud volunteer for Crisis Text Line—a nonprofit organization offering free text-based mental health support and crisis intervention. Helping others through emotional experiences is both a talent and passion of hers.

At the age of fifteen, Richards discovered her joy for writing. She began writing poetry to help cope with her emotional burdens and escape reality. Now, she is basking in the opportunity to combine writing and helping others into one venue. In her much-coveted free time, she enjoys traveling, crafting, DIY projects, and reading all the books. For pretty pictures of books and recommendations, follow her on Instagram @bookedwithscarlett.

E. K. Richards still resides in Utah, where her blended family and fur babies are building a life they love together.

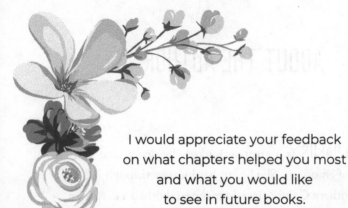

I would appreciate your feedback
on what chapters helped you most
and what you would like
to see in future books.

If you enjoyed this book and
found it helpful, please
leave a **REVIEW** on Amazon.

Visit me at

EKRICHARDS.COM

where you can learn more about me
and my many passion projects.

Thank You!